CLERICALISM

CLERICALISM

THE INSTITUTIONAL DIMENSION OF THE CATHOLIC SEXUAL ABUSE CRISIS

C. Colt Anderson
with J. D. Long García

Paulist Press
New York / Mahwah, NJ

Cover image by tomeqs/Shutterstock.com
Cover and book design by Lynn Else

Library of Congress Cataloging-in-Publication Data
Names: Anderson, C. Colt author | Long García, J. D. author
Title: Clericalism: the institutional dimension of the Catholic sexual abuse crisis / C. Colt Anderson, with J. D. Long García.
Description: Mahwah, NJ: Paulist Press, [2026] | Includes index. | Summary: "This book identifies the rules and incentives that have prevented the Catholic Church from implementing sustainable reforms regarding sexual abuse and identifies a way forward"—Provided by publisher.
Identifiers: LCCN 2025030166 (print) | LCCN 2025030167 (ebook) | ISBN 9780809157808 paperback | ISBN 9780809189496 ebook
Subjects: LCSH: Catholic Church—Government | Clericalism | Catholic Church—Clergy—Sexual behavior | Child sexual abuse by clergy
Classification: LCC BX1803. A53 2026 (print) | LCC BX1803 (ebook)
LC record available at https://lccn.loc.gov/2025030166
LC ebook record available at https://lccn.loc.gov/2025030167

ISBN 978-0-8091-5780-8 (paperback)
ISBN 978-0-8091-8949-6 (ebook)

Published by Paulist Press
997 Macarthur Boulevard
Mahwah, NJ 07430
www.paulistpress.com

Printed and bound in the
United States of America

CONTENTS

PREFACE

One of the central aims of this book is to explain why the Catholic Church—why we—are trapped in a dynamic that is sapping away our credibility as an organization. This dynamic, which we call the clericalism trap, is deeply rooted in church history and is fed by the need to project an image of holiness, even perfection, to justify the authority and independence of the clergy. This trap remains in place, and the church cannot fulfill its mission of sharing the love of Christ without uprooting it. Having identified the trap, we cannot help but warn others of its existence.

To that end, another goal is to point to strategies for escaping the trap we have constructed for ourselves. Exploring the divine element of the church, which is perfect, is not our objective; instead, we are studying the human element, which is not perfect. In short, we are investigating what has traditionally been identified as the institutional church or the church as an organization or a society. To do so, we are drawing on theology, history, and economics to surface some institutional deficiencies that need reform.

We want to explain who we are and why we have written this book. This is not a disinterested study of clericalism and institutional reform. J. D. Long García and I are active members of the Catholic Church who have worked for the church in different capacities over most of our careers. We began this book with one question in mind: "Why is it that the Catholic Church seems unable to respond effectively to the sexual abuse crisis?" When we say that the church has been unable to respond effectively, we do not mean to deny progress. There are dioceses, orders, and Catholic organizations that have improved their implementation, oversight, and enforcement of norms to protect children. Most of the people we interviewed for our study were hopeful and pointed to progress in the ways that their local diocese or province had implemented training or processes for reporting accusations of child sexual abuse to the authorities. When people pointed to progress, they reported being aware of issues in neighboring dioceses, provinces, or orders. Where there is progress, it is due to the commitment, knowledge, and character of a local ordinary or superior.

There is much at stake. Good progress is all too frequently dependent on the outside scrutiny that comes from the media, attorneys general, and judges. In our contemporary media environment, a failure in any diocese or religious order implicates the whole church in the minds of Catholics. Each failure results in more Catholics being scandalized. With every new report of priestly sexual abuse, the authority of priests and bishops is diminished further.

Even though the Catholic Church is much greater than the sum of its ordained clergy, the misdeeds of the ordained impact everyone. In a pluralistic society, there is a very low cost to exit the Catholic Church, especially when poor and unaccountable leadership has so fundamentally undermined its moral credibility. The problem has been made worse by the fact that the magisterium has taught that the church's authority is derived from its holiness and perfection. The magisterium has identified itself as the necessary mediator of the true source of holiness—the grace of the Holy Spirit found in the bonds of love in a Christian community. For much of the last five hundred years, the bishops have failed to listen to the critiques of their leadership and governance, insisting instead on their total independence from any accountability to the laity. The results are unacceptable.

If the bishops fail to give voice to their internal critics in meaningful ways—the power to influence change from within—they cannot expect to maintain loyalty.[1] The same critique can be made concerning the religious superiors who pay insufficient attention to the critiques of the people assisting them in running their various ministries as well as those of the people they serve. Though Pope Francis called for the clergy to listen to the laity in a synodal process, he denied the laity any role in governance. Francis's intent was laudable, but many people have concluded that the Catholic Church will never reform itself without changing how it understands whose voices matter. The propensity to simply exit an organization that both asserts its perfection and denies the possibility of change is apparent when one considers that the Catholic Church has lost more members in the last fifty years to disaffiliation in just the United States than it lost during the Protestant Reformation.

The church is not becoming purer as its membership diminishes; instead, we are losing the capacity to be a sign of salvation. Those who remain are the most loyal members, and we are seeking to encourage this remnant to bring their insights and wisdom to bear on the problem of clericalism and its effects. We write because we want the Catholic Church to thrive and not merely survive. To provide context for our work, we will briefly explain how we came to this project individually.

C. COLT ANDERSON

Before I present my theological background, I want to admit that I am deeply grateful for the assistance I have received from the Catholic Church. I grew up with a single mother and a nonsupportive father from the late 1960s to the early 1980s, meaning we were poor. The Franciscan sisters in Savannah educated me for free when I was young, at least until we were evicted from our apartment and had to move. Later the Sisters of Mercy came to our aid. I should also mention that many Methodists and Baptists helped us over the years. As the Catholic Church loses the capacity to act effectively in the world, I imagine all the people who are slipping through the increasingly big holes in the social safety net just as our ability to respond as a church to people's needs diminishes.

My path out of poverty would be unlikely today.

This book represents the culmination of more than twenty years of studying and writing about the history of reform in the Catholic Church. I write as a Catholic theologian speaking from my faith as well as my experience as a seminary professor, a member of an apostolic visitation of seminaries, a dean of a seminary, and a dean of a graduate school of religion. While I am opposed to clericalism, I am not opposed to the ordained clergy. I have worked with, trained, and taught many priests and bishops. I found many of them admirable, and there are more than a few whom I can say I loved. This book is not about them except insofar as we are all caught in the trap of clericalism together. We hope that we can remove the impediments—the stumbling blocks—preventing us from fully manifesting the gospel by lifting people up both materially and spiritually. Clericalism is robbing us of our capacity to help the poor, to provide education, to evangelize, and to advocate for the oppressed.

Although the Jesuits trained me and I work in a Jesuit university, I most closely identify with the Franciscan school of thought as expressed by St. Bonaventure. I am following in the footsteps of the *ressourcement* theologians like my friend and mentor George Tavard, AA, who was a student of Henri de Lubac, SJ, and a *peritus* at the Second Vatican Council. The *ressourcement* movement emerged out of the French schools of theology in France during the first half of the twentieth century as an alternative to the rigid neo-Scholasticism that dominated Catholic theology in the seminaries and universities. *Ressourcement* theologians sought to address contemporary issues in the church by recovering theology from the early and medieval church.

Tavard taught me that the Catholic Church values precedents and that I would need to ground my theology in sources such as the writings of the saints, the doctors of the church, and ecumenical councils in order to be taken seriously. At the same time, he taught me that it is necessary to discern between history and tradition, as they are frequently conflated, resulting in doctrinal corruption. Because Catholics tend to invest too much authority in canon law, he emphasized that theologians should be mindful that most canon law is positive law as opposed to natural or divine law. Positive law can and should change according to the circumstances. Most importantly, he stressed the importance of the principle that what has changed in the Catholic Church can change, which is particularly important when thinking about church governance.

Wanda Cizewski, who directed my dissertation, instilled in me an appreciation of close historical research and the work of Marie-Dominque Chenu, OP, who cofounded the Pontifical Medieval Institute at the University of Toronto. Chenu believed the goal of historical theology is to understand the social entities and factors that underlie texts, controversies, systems, and doctrines. His appreciation for the social sciences and their importance for understanding the church inspired me to familiarize myself with writers in anthropology, sociology, political science, and economics.

My first book studied how Bonaventure and the Friars Minor struggled to implement the pastoral care reforms of the Fourth Lateran Council (1215) while maintaining fidelity to Francis of Assisi's Rule of 1223.[2] Bonaventure compared the church to the moon to explain how it waxes and wanes in terms of its holiness. He told his brothers that there are times when sin and failure almost totally obscure the church, but even then, like the moon, it is still there and exerting its influence on the tides of history. Bonaventure assured his brothers that the church would grow brighter after the period of darkness in which they were living.[3]

When the stories began to emerge from Boston, I drew upon Bonaventure to explain how you can speak of communal sin in order to call for communal conversion. He described the church as repeatedly returning to its own original sin—legalism—throughout history. Bonaventure defined this legalism as the attempt to take something granted by the church, such as an office, a ministry, or a charism, and claim it as one's own. When people see their power and position as their personal property, they assert their rights over the good of the community.[4] Bonaventure's understanding of legalism provided me with a lens for examining how clericalism, understood as a sin, had undermined the policy passed by the U.S. Conference of Catholic Bishops in 1992 to remove priests who had been credibly accused of the sexual abuse of a minor. I saw Bonaventure's theology as providing a warning that the Dallas Charter, the U.S. bishops' response in 2002 to the sexual abuse crisis, was likely to fail without establishing some form of accountability for the bishops.

Later, I began to believe that the effort to call the bishops away from clericalism, still understood as a sin, was insufficient. I found another model in the writing of St. Peter Damian, who is the Doctor of Reform. Peter Damian advocated for a legal approach to the abuses associated with simony, clerical concubinage, and sexual abuse of minors. Proper order, according to this saint, particularly demands that the worst offenses need to be made public. On one level, he was simply echoing the penitential disciplines of the ancient and medieval church, but on another level, he was arguing that publicly revealing the worst sins was the means to preserve the credibility of the church.

If the church exposed the worst offenses, Peter Damian concluded that it would reveal all sins. Conversely, when the church is lax in its discipline and hushes up the worst sins of its members, it signals that it is not serious about its own laws, tradition, and mission. The worse the church does in terms of presenting a bad example of Christian order, the more it undermines its ability to save souls and diminishes its authority. This laxity, he argued, stood in direct contradiction to Jesus's teaching on the importance of following the law in Matthew 5:19.[5] Peter Damian formulated the principle that the sins of more highly placed people must be more vigorously prosecuted than those of the anonymous and powerless. He argued that this is how God punishes sinners, citing Numbers 25:4: "And the Lord was angry and said to Moses, 'Take all of the leaders of the people and hang them on gallows in the full light of day, that the fury of my anger may turn away from Israel.'"[6]

As I worked on *The Great Catholic Reformers: From Gregory the Great to Dorothy Day*, I drew on another *ressourcement* theologian, Yves Congar, OP, who had written about distinguishing between true and false reform in the church. I came to see how the efforts at reform using a pastoral care approach failed to establish sustainable reforms. Further, the efforts to change the church through canon law were unsuccessful because there was no consistent enforcement. Humanists in the sixteenth century recognized how systems or structures in the church needed to change, but once the Council of Trent implemented several structural reforms, the popes and the bishops abandoned the cause of reform in favor of promoting the perfection of the Catholic Church. When I completed the reformers book, I knew that there was a problem with how we understand discipline and accountability, but I did not have the language or categories I needed to analyze the problem or suggest how to move forward.

After publishing a series of chapters on different aspects of reform in the Middle Ages, I was invited to participate in a grant considering how to respond to the rise of religious nationalism. The Wagner School of Public Policy at New York University invited me as a visiting scholar to facilitate the research. As I was working on the project, I was also researching the question of whether or not we could call some of the fifteenth-century humanists at the Council of Constance institutional reformers. I asked my colleague, David Elcott, to provide me with some sources from the public policy world that examined institutional reform to gain another perspective. He introduced me to the work of the economist Douglass North, which finally gave me a way to understand why reforms in the Middle Ages were unsuccessful. I also began to see how North's "institutional analysis" seemed applicable to the sexual abuse crisis.

As I was becoming familiar with institutional change in the public policy sector, corporations, and school districts, the Theology Department and The Francis and Ann Curran Center for American Catholic Studies at Fordham University launched the Taking Responsibility Initiative. The initiative invited researchers to study the conditions that foster the sexual abuse of vulnerable people and its concealment in Roman Catholic and Jesuit schools, colleges, and universities. With the help of a professor of economics, Henry Schwalbenberg, and a professor of management sciences, Michael Pirson, I came up with a grant proposal that allowed me to hire a research assistant and to conduct interviews to assess the applicability of institutional analysis for studying the persistent failures in ecclesial administration or governance. While holding interviews, my assistant, J. D. Long García, and I came across a wealth of information indicating the church desperately needs institutional reforms. Further, these institutions or rules also impact other disciplinary problems. Because the research included analyzing and reporting on interviews in addition to historical and theological analysis, I invited my assistant, who is an accomplished journalist and a doctoral candidate, to coauthor this book.

J. D. LONG GARCÍA

I was in graduate school in 2002 when the *Boston Globe* broke the story about sexual abuse in the Catholic Church. A year later, revelations about my home diocese of Phoenix emerged. The bishop, Thomas O'Brien, resigned after a fatal hit-and-run accident. Little did I know then that I would end up working for the Diocese of Phoenix the following year. I was hired as the bilingual managing editor of the diocesan publication, and I've been working in Catholic media ever since.

Less than a year after I started working for the diocese, survivors credibly accused the pastor of my parish. One of my pastor's victims called my office distraught because my pastor had started a new church in his neighborhood. He was in tears. I heard him out but explained that I had little power to do anything about it. I certainly couldn't report on it for the paper. Diocesan lawyers told newspaper staff members we couldn't write about it. The bishop was the publisher, and the lawyers told us that had legal implications.

About six years later, survivors came forward with credible accusations against my pastor's replacement. My boss told me about it at a Catholic Media Conference we were attending. In our pages, we published a community notification note written by the diocesan legal counsel. Not long after, one of the survivors' fathers called my office one night, probably expecting to get my voicemail, but I was working late. His son, who our new pastor had abused, had committed suicide. He blamed the pastor. Like the survivor who had called years before, this father was also in tears. He felt the community notification, which glossed over the accusations against our new pastor, was an insult to his son's memory. I apologized but had to explain that as much as I'd like to write more about it, I could not. My firstborn son was about four years old at the time, so hearing another father's grief about his child being abused pierced my heart.

Those of us who work for the Roman Catholic Church are familiar with Safe Environment Training. It tends to get mixed reviews. I've heard fellow parishioners complain about the amount of time they spend on sexual abuse prevention when they're just trying to volunteer as, for example, a lector. But my experience of the training may be a little bit different. As I sat in the multipurpose room, watching the video with others about predators' grooming techniques, I started thinking of my confirmation sponsor.

Mr. A. was my school counselor at the high school I attended. He was kind and seemed to get a kick out of my multicultural upbringing. I was born in the Dominican Republic to a Dominican mother and an American father. I've been told I look more like my father. Mr. A. encouraged me to attend high school support groups he led for Latino kids. He seemed particularly delighted when I attended Spanish-language groups and surprised other Latino kids by speaking fluent Spanish, albeit with a Dominican accent. As he was my confirmation sponsor, I didn't think twice when he offered to take me out to eat or for a visit to the local fair. Eventually, he invited me to his home where—I learned the word a decade later—he molested me.

Sitting in that safe environment training, the memories of it all came back to me. I simply hadn't thought about it for years. I brushed it off as Mr. A. simply being peculiar, perhaps overly affectionate. But at that moment, I recognized what I may not have been able to admit to myself at the time. That he crossed a line. And that he intended to do far worse. I reported it to the diocesan victims' advocate once I realized what had happened. "Do you intend to press charges against the church?" That was among the first questions she asked me. "What? No…I just thought I should tell someone. In case he's still sponsoring kids in confirmation…." I met with her, and she set me up with a counselor. She explained that the kind of physical contact Mr. A. had with me was the same as what my old pastor did with his victims. It was a step to more. I was fortunate it hadn't gone further, she said. Her words didn't sit right. I know now that he was grooming me.

I shared the experience with a couple of family members, but no one else. I certainly didn't write about it at the time. Years later, I wrote a report on a possible sexual reckoning among the Latino community and a column about not letting the sexual abuse crisis lead to homophobia.[7] Sex abuse by clergy was a topic of many conversations at the V Encuentro

National Gathering in late September of 2018, which I covered for *America* magazine. That summer, media outlets reported on Cardinal Theodore E. McCarrick's sexual abuse of minors. What emerged as I spoke with Latino conference attendees was a distinctly different reaction from the Anglo community. Where vocal Anglo Catholics tended to blame the bishops for the ongoing abuse, Latino Catholics showed their support to the bishops and offered to help however they could.

Latino Catholics tend to support the clergy, Boston College's Hosffman Ospino told me in an interview that summer.[8] "The tone was different," he said. "It's not that they were naïve because they're immigrants. But this cultural Catholicism somehow invites responses that also involve prayer, forgiveness, and reconciliation."[9] Right or wrong, the reaction from Latino Catholics planted a question. Do the bishops even have the capacity to handle the sexual abuse crisis? I explored that question further in an opinion piece I wrote after the release of the McCarrick Report.[10] There, I revealed my own experience of abuse and, as a father of children, questioned whether the bishops should oversee the response to the sexual abuse crisis at all.

The typical reactions to the report—which again put the blame on the bishops and focused on what the episcopate could do to fix things—frustrated me. It felt like an endless cycle. I wrote, "When it comes to sexual abuse, the wrong people are in charge. If we continue to expect bishops to take care of this for us, we perpetuate a fundamental problem. We enable clericalism. We must set that aside and take over."[11] At that time, I had been working for several months with Colt Anderson as his research assistant. His analysis of the sexual abuse crisis in the Catholic Church had already influenced me. Other explanations of the crisis felt incomplete, and in working on the project, I began to understand why. He invited me to the assistantship, in part, because of my background in industrial and organizational psychology, which I studied at a graduate level. To complete my degree, I designed a descriptive phenomenological study of authentic leadership. This experience in qualitative research, textual analysis, and I/O psychology supported the study. It is a deeply personal project, not only because of my own experience with abuse, but because I am a devout Catholic and a father. I want my children to be safe within the walls of our Catholic Church. I believe in the fullness of the life of faith that is offered through the sacraments. Future generations should at least consider the richness of the life offered by the church. But simply wishing it will not make it so. The sins of the past must be redressed. That still has not happened.

Elie Wiesel, in his 1986 Nobel Prize acceptance speech, recalled how the world knew about the horrors of Nazi Germany and remained silent. "And that is why I swore never to be silent whenever and wherever human beings endure suffering and humiliation. We must take sides. Neutrality helps the oppressor, never the victim. Silence encourages the tormentor, never the tormented. Sometimes we must interfere."[12] Our study reveals not only a propensity to silence throughout the Catholic Church, but also structures and institutions that perpetuate it. Our church must be reformed.

CLERICALISM AND ABUSE

Clericalism, which we define as the idealization of priests and the Catholic Church as an organization, hurts everyone. Maintaining a façade of perfection demands a lot of energy and effort to conceal serious failures on the part of individual priests and bishops. Clericalism also hurts the priests and bishops by placing an unbearable burden of perfection on them, causing many to withdraw from healthy relationships within the communities they serve lest people see their flaws. Concealing failures, such as the sexual abuse of vulnerable people, facilitates the abuses of predators and complicates the ministry of the rest of the clergy. Clericalism creates the conditions for scandal and shatters trust.

As we shall see, the patterns of behavior and incentives that have emerged from clericalism have deep historical roots that have been undermining our capacity to implement sustainable reforms by creating incentives to conceal sexual abuse and other crimes.[13] The problem of sexual abuse in the church is not new. What is new is that it has become virtually impossible in many parts of the world to cover up such crimes, given advances in communication technologies and a greater willingness to talk about sexual matters. While concealing and minimizing abuse was a strategy that served to enhance the Catholic Church's authority and independence from the Middle Ages until the Industrial Age, the Information Age calls for a strategy that is more consistent with St. Paul's exhortation to the Ephesians: "For once you were darkness, but now in the Lord you are light. Live as children of light—for the fruit of the light is found in all that is good and right and true. Try to find out what is pleasing to the Lord. Take no part in the unfruitful works of darkness, but instead expose them" (Eph 5:8–11).[14]

ACKNOWLEDGMENTS

There are many people who helped us bring this book to fruition. First, we want to thank our families for allowing us the time to complete this project. Our spouses, Rose Anderson and Tamara Long García, have had to make sacrifices so that we had the time to research, write, and edit this book. They have read drafts and provided helpful suggestions and encouragement during this six-year endeavor. We also recognize that our children, Rachel and Kristen Anderson, as well as Lukas, Manuel Santiago, and Mora María Long García, have had less time with us than either we or they would like. We hope our work will help the Catholic Church become safer and healthier for our children, whether they are young like Long García's family or young adults in Anderson's family.

We are also grateful to the Fordham Taking Responsibility Initiative, which provided funding to learn more about the structural and cultural features of Jesuit educational institutions that facilitate both sexual abuse and its concealment. Bradford Hinze and Christine Hinze, who were central to the Taking Responsibility Initiative, helped us to adjust as we had to contend with the pandemic and its fallout on the interview process. Catherine Osborne, who coordinated the initiative, was always ready to help and was a valuable partner in the research process.

Of course, there would be no book without the people who agreed to be interviewed. We appreciate their generosity and their deep desire to help the Catholic Church fulfill its mission. Their sense of urgency to break the cycle of abuse informs this volume. We felt a great responsibility to the participants to make sure their voices would be heard.

We also want to thank the people who read the chapters and provided us with feedback. John Seitz and Sónia da Silva Monteiro from Fordham Department of Theology helped us clarify the introduction and the first chapter. Two ecclesiologists, John Burkhard, OFM Conv, and Michael Canaris, reviewed some of the earlier chapters and were valuable conversation partners around matters touching on apostolic and nonapostolic traditions. Eileen Burchell, who is a retired professor from Fordham and an excellent writer, read most of the book for its comprehensibility to the nonexpert.

Three of the graduates of Fordham's doctor of ministry program read pieces of the book: Don Kremer, Deacon Paul St. Laurent, and Caterina Mako. They helped us achieve greater clarity at several points along the way. All three have worked or are working in the church and they confirmed that the dynamics we were describing in the sections they read resonated with their experiences.

Finally, we want to thank Christopher Bellitto for editing the book. We brought the book to Paulist Press first so that we might work with him. It is fitting since Bellitto asked the question that started this journey. He asked Anderson to present a paper considering whether or not fifteenth-century humanists were "institutional reformers" for the American Cusanus Society. He also edited Anderson's *The Great Catholic Reformers: From Gregory the Great to Dorothy Day* (Paulist Press, 2007) and this book picks up where the earlier study left off. Bellitto has skillfully sharpened our manuscript into the book before you.

CHAPTER 1

CHANGING THE RULES OF THE GAME

While there are significant problems, we do recognize that there are many outstanding bishops, priests, deacons, religious, and lay employees who are doing more than their share of the work to manifest the church's sacramental nature. Moreover, there are many lay Catholics who provide service to the poor, who fight for justice, and who witness to the gospel. We are focusing this study, however, on the ways we fall short of this task as a result of clericalism and the rules it generates. While such a focus can be uncomfortable, we believe it is necessary to honestly and forthrightly take account of our failures so that we can amend them.

If we want to make progress on the sexual abuse scandal and the associated breakdown in proper order, then we must move from the pastoral care model of reform to institutional reform in the church. To do so, we must rethink how we understand institutions and their relationship to pastoral care. This task is complicated by the fact that institutions have a sacred connotation for many Catholics. The magisterium places a great deal of emphasis on the fact that Christ instituted the priesthood, hierarchy, the office of bishops, and so forth. These formulations are historically problematic on several levels; nonetheless, they are the source of the sacred understanding of ecclesial institutions. We want to state at the outset we are not using the term *institution* to refer to sacraments, priesthood, or hierarchy.

The word *institution* has multiple meanings in the fields we employ. Institutions can indicate the type of rules associated with the founding of religious orders. Institutions can also designate offices, organizations, and structures. The institutional analysis we are doing, which is drawn from the work of the Nobel Prize–winning economist Douglass C. North, defines *institutions* as the formal and informal rules that organize social, political, and economic relations. In a paper for the United Nations Economic Commission for Europe, he described institutional analysis this way:

> What we are concerned with is the cultural heritage of humans. By that I mean something very specific; I mean a set of institutions and beliefs that has been carried forward over the generations that constitutes the basic way we perceive the world. We have a very limited ability to change it; it is path dependent in the sense that the inheritance we have of rules, norms, beliefs—those that have survived—is deeply embedded. Sometimes the embeddedness is deeper than at other times but it poses a genuine problem because that cultural heritage produces a mix of good and bad that shapes the way in which we make choices and the ways in which societies and institutions evolve.[1]

Institutions are the societal rules or "the humanly devised constraints that shape human interaction."[2] They serve the important purpose of reducing uncertainty in terms of how people interact with each other, which allows them to plan.

We found North's research appropriate for three reasons. First, his definition of *institutions* is widely accepted in the social sciences, including economics, political science, and sociology. Second, North's understanding of institutions is used by international organizations and development agencies such as the United Nations and the World Bank because it is helpful for understanding why reform efforts frequently fail and how to avoid those failures. Finally, his work is applicable to church history and theology since he was an economic historian whose method incorporated contextual concerns such as beliefs.

North called the formal and informal institutions in an organization the rules of the game. These rules create incentives and disincentives for behavior within an organization. *Organization* is a broad term that can include states, corporations, businesses, nonprofits, local governments, and religious groups. Formal institutions are usually expressed in written policies, constitutions, charters, and laws; however, laws, charters, and policies are not necessarily institutions. Changing a law or policy does not indicate institutional reform because not all laws are rules. A law is only a rule or an institution when it has become internalized, customary, and normative. Informal institutions can be found in methods of operation, undocumented norms, unwritten traditions, rules governing client-patron chains, and patrimonial political relationships. An organization with many informal institutions, such as the Catholic Church, is particularly well-adapted to undermine changes to laws, policies, and charters.[3]

Obviously, the formal and informal institutions do not incentivize the sexual abuse of minors or other people; however, they do guide how all Catholics perceive events and respond to them. We say all Catholics because many of these institutions extend to the religious and the laity. One rule that we think most readers will recognize is that you must treat a priest or bishop differently than everyone else. In many cases, this differential is expressed in terms of etiquette. For example, when Cardinal George opened a homily at an ordination that filled the chapel at the seminary—a crowd of roughly six hundred—he said that he could count the number of people of goodwill in the Archdiocese of Chicago on two hands. But since he was the cardinal archbishop, no one pointed out that this was a stupid and insensitive thing to say to the families of the men being ordained in attendance—not to mention assembled clergy, faculty, and sponsors.

The power differential is more insidious for those who work either directly for a diocese or in an organization sponsored by Catholic dioceses or religious orders. The ordained do not have to follow the policies or meet the expectations required for other employees in Catholic organizations such as dioceses, schools, and universities. Dioceses establish priest personnel boards that follow different procedures from those of their human resources departments. These boards keep records that are separate from other personnel and are held strictly confidential. When the annual audits called for by the Dallas Charter take place, the auditors are not given access to the priest personnel boards or even seminary files.[4] This practice reflects the ideology that priests are so separate and superior to everyone else that a different set of rules applies to them.

The separateness and superiority of the *priest*, which is a term that can also indicate a bishop, is deeply rooted in Catholic history; however, as we shall see, it is neither scriptural nor a part of the apostolic tradition.

The claim that priests should be separate and superior originated in the reform rhetoric of the eleventh century, which also aimed at liberating the clergy from accountability to the laity. The apologetics and polemics of popes and their supporters advanced the idea that the clerical state is perfect—even if some members are not—and thus the clergy is as a group superior to the laity.

These papal apologists grounded the superiority of the priests in their sacred role or function rather than in some idea of ontological change, which only emerged in Catholic circles after the Second Vatican Council. Pastoral ministry was the source of their status. At the same time, they affirmed that pastoral ministry required a greater degree of ritual purity. Given their superior role, these apologists argued they should be independent of all forms of accountability to the lay authorities. Justifying their authority and independence in claims to perfection and holiness created powerful incentives to conceal the crimes of priests and bishops. It is this idealization of the clergy that has created the clericalism trap.

Clericalism is frequently invoked as one of the primary causes of the sexual abuse crisis in recent magisterial documents. These documents describe clericalism as a sin on the part of individual priests and bishops. In his 2018 postsynodal exhortation, *Christus Vivit*, Francis wrote, "Clericalism is a constant temptation on the part of priests who see 'the ministry they have received as a power to be exercised, rather than a free and generous service to be offered.'"[5] The Congregation for the Clergy's 2016 *Ratio Fundamentalis*, which guides formation in seminary programs, also categorizes clericalism as a species of pride or presumption affecting priests.[6] However, identifying clericalism as a species of pride on the part of individual clerics is a form of the "few bad apples" apologetic that the magisterium has employed since the papacy of Leo XIII.[7]

Defining *clericalism* as a sin indicates the proper response is through pastoral care reform. As a pastoral issue, clericalism implies that it is a problem for the clergy to resolve and implicitly denies the competence of the laity to address it. Pastoral care emphasizes patience and mercy with the goal of reconciliation. It protects the privacy of sinners using terms such as *charitable discretion* and *fraternal correction*, which also serves to create a culture of concealment. Certainly, sin is an aspect of the crisis, but it does not explain why the problem of sexual abuse is so pervasive and persistent except insofar as sin can be invoked to explain all the evils of the world. Starting from sin obscures the institutions, structures, and systems contributing to the crisis.

Rather than defining *clericalism* in terms of sin, we use the definition employed by the Australian Royal Commission into Institutional Responses to Child Sexual Abuse. It defined *clericalism* as "the idealization of the priesthood, and by extension, the idealization of the Catholic Church."[8] The commission made a case that this idealization fostered the sense of entitlement, superiority, and exclusion that created the conditions for abuses of power. Clericalism also nurtured the idea that the Catholic Church was autonomous and self-sufficient to handle these crimes.[9] The commission concluded this "culture of clericalism" motivated church leaders to avoid public scandals that could undermine the status of the priesthood and thus the reputation of the church.[10]

The Australian Royal Commission's definition is consistent with an older way of understanding clericalism. Cardinal Avery Dulles critiqued what he described as an institutionalist ecclesiology that understood the church as totally clerical with the ordained being responsible for teaching, sanctifying, and ruling the laity. He believed it gave rise to clericalism or the attempt to reduce the role of the laity to complete passivity.[11] Those who support this ecclesiology, Dulles explained, identify the church itself with the members of the hierarchy.[12]

The tendency to identify the church with the members of the ordained hierarchy is echoed in the ways that even progressive Catholics speak about "the church" when they mean the bishops or the magisterium. Even the way we use the term *hierarchy* has been influenced by clericalism. Pseudo-Dionysius the Areopagite, who created the term, included the laity in the ecclesiastical hierarchy.[13] Doctors of the church like Thomas Aquinas and Robert Bellarmine also included the laity in the ecclesiastical hierarchy.[14] One of those doctors, Bonaventure, ascribed the primacy of the Father to the laity, noting that the clergy and the religious come from the laity.[15] Yet Vatican II sharply distinguished the laity from the hierarchy.[16]

Recognizing clericalism as an ideology that has developed over time opens avenues for reform beyond praying for "a continuous and profound conversion of hearts," as Pope Francis put it.[17] Catholics must shift their thinking about the church from "them"—meaning the bishops—to "us" to break out of the vicious cycle created by the idealization of the priesthood and the identification of the priesthood with the church; however, this will not happen as the result of widespread and spontaneous metanoia. Instead, we need to analyze where we have gone wrong as a community and take a problem-solving approach to those failures. Our research aimed to identify where the disciplinary process was breaking down given that there were already canons in place that were not enforced prior to the publicity of the sexual abuse crisis.

Though we were studying the rules that foster the sexual abuse of vulnerable people in Catholic and Jesuit schools, colleges, and universities, the rules we found also have implications for other disciplinary issues such as financial improprieties, substance abuse, and failure to perform one's duties. This book addresses the broader implications of institutional defects in addition to warning Catholics to avoid the temptation to believe that these problems will be resolved by changes to canon law or that a reforming pope can revise the formal and informal institutions by fiat. Such a belief is not a sign of hope but rather a form of wishful thinking, which raises expectations of easy solutions.

This is not to say that a reforming pope can have no effect or that pastoral care rules are irrelevant. A reforming pope can use pastoral care principles to change the narrative. Changing the narrative is necessary for institutional reform to take place. The legal scholar Robert M. Cover explained the relationship between narrative and institutions this way:

> We inhabit a *nomos*—a normative universe. We constantly create and maintain a world of right and wrong, of lawful and unlawful, of valid and void. The student of law may come to identify the normative world with the professional paraphernalia of social control. The rules and principles of justice, the formal institutions of the law, and the conventions of a social order are, indeed, important to that world; they are, however, but a small part of the normative universe that ought to claim our attention. No set of legal institutions or prescriptions exists apart from the narratives that locate it and give it meaning. For every constitution there is an epic, for each Decalogue a scripture. Once understood in the context of the narratives that give it meaning, law becomes not merely a system of rules to be observed, but a world in which we live.[18]

Law and narrative are inseparably related in this *nomos*. Any effective change to the institutional rules relies on a change of narrative as well as mechanisms of enforcement by third-party organizations. Pope Francis was right to call attention to the need for conversion and for providing better pastoral care, but the Catholic Church urgently needs institutional change.

At the same time, pastoral care rules are part of the problem because they have been identified with governance, administration, and canon law. The church has a mission and pastoral care or the care of souls is a vital aspect of its mission, but there are other aspects as well. The mission of the church is addressed in each of the three models of the church that the Second Vatican presents in *Lumen Gentium*: church as mystery, church as people of God, and church as hierarchy.

Lumen Gentium explained what it means to consider the church a mystery. The document defined the church's mission as being a "sacrament or instrumental sign of intimate union with God and of the unity of all humanity."[19] The church is the kingdom of Christ already present in mystery and grows through the power of God. The Holy Spirit leads the church into all truth and makes it one in fellowship and ministry, according to the council, by directing it through a diversity of gifts, both hierarchical and charismatic, so that it can serve as an instrumental sign (*LG* 4).

The description of the church's mission in the chapter on the people of God is consonant with the previous chapter. The council declared, "God has called together the assembly of those who look to Jesus in faith as the author of salvation and the principle of unity and peace, and has constituted the church that it may be for one and all the visible sacrament of this saving unity" (*LG* 9). The persistent problems of corruption and scandal—not to mention the incompetence and mediocrity Catholics frequently encounter in parishes, dioceses, and other organizations in the church—obscure the church as a sacrament of saving unity.

The discussion of the church's mission shifts in chapter 3 of *Lumen Gentium* to the mission of the bishops. Here the council speaks of ministers endowed with sacred power who are directed to promoting the good of the whole body (*LG* 18). The council teaches that Jesus Christ willed that the successors to the apostles, the bishops, should be shepherds (*pastores*) until the consummation of the world (*LG* 18). "These shepherds, chosen to nourish the Lord's flock," the council explained, "are the ministers of Christ and the dispensers of the mysteries of God, to whom has been entrusted the bearing of witness to the gospel of God's grace, and the service of the Spirit and of justice in glory" (*LG* 21). In addition to the tasks of preaching and providing sacramental ministry, the bishops are given the task of governing the churches entrusted to them. The council did not describe their governance in detail, but it stressed that this power is exercised personally in the name of Christ and that only the pope can circumscribe it "within certain limits for the good of the church or the faithful" (*LG* 27). The limits of episcopal power are not defined.

Whereas chapter 3 of *Lumen Gentium* in isolation would suggest that pastoral ministry is the mission of the church, the previous two chapters remind us that such ministry is just one of the ways that the church fulfills its mission. Even pastoral ministry has three distinct functions: teaching or preaching, dispensing sacraments, and governing. Moreover, it is not the only form of ministry in the church. The Second Vatican pointed to Ephesians 4:11–12 and 1 Corinthians 12:4 to indicate the diversity of gifts, services, and activities in the church. St. Paul identified different "offices" or roles performed by apostles, prophets, evangelists, pastors, and teachers. The early church recognized there is a significant difference between pastoral care, which focuses on serving the converted, and evangelization, which reaches out to those who are either ignorant of or hostile to the faith.[20]

Exactly what the roles of each of these ministries were in the apostolic era is far from clear, but St. Paul distinguished pastoral care, teaching, and evangelizing as different forms of service or activity to equip the saints for the work of ministry. Just looking at the threefold role of priest, prophet, and king of the baptized indicates that pastoral principles cannot guide all decisions in the church. Prophets have the role of speaking truth to the power of the priests and kings. Kings have the role of protecting their people and administering justice. Priests have the role of offering forgiveness, providing sacraments, and building unity. Even if bishops and religious superiors can function equally as a priest, prophet, and king simultaneously, which is far from clear to us, they should not allow the pastoral aim of reconciliation to supplant the kingly goal of providing justice and security for the community. Someone can be forgiven and, nonetheless, be unfit to hold office in the church.

The rules related to pastoral care principles impact how policies and provisions of canon law are applied throughout Catholic organizations. Some of these rules are codified in law and policy, but some are informal and are transmitted through traditions and customary procedures. The informal rules guide how—and even whether—law and policy are applied. They provide insight into the difference between what a law, policy, or charter states and what is actually done. Unsurprisingly, these rules also guide the intellectual, spiritual, and human formation process in the seminaries.

An example of how informal rules undermine discipline can be seen in the way that bishops transfer men who have been confronted with serious academic or moral problems by the seminary faculty and administrators. There is a prudent policy requiring a two-year period of probation after a seminarian is officially dismissed from a seminary before he can enter another program, but the informal rule is that seminarians should be allowed to withdraw before being dismissed, ostensibly in order to save them embarrassment. Because seminaries rarely formally dismiss men, bishops can move these men to another seminary immediately without violating the policy, which was approved by Rome.

The informal rules also impact decisions in dioceses and Catholic organizations that operate on a national level. They dictate how clergy, as well as lay and religious employees, are assessed and disciplined in many if not most Catholic organizations. While the process is different for lay employees, the clergy who make the final decisions frequently fall back on pastoral principles of sheltering people from embarrassment, protecting privacy, and being merciful. Moreover, our interviews revealed the emphasis placed on mercy varies in terms of how close the employees are to their priestly supervisors.

In order to identify the rules (institutions) that were determining how canon law and organizational policies are applied, we consulted with a professor of economics and a professor of management sciences to devise a list of questions to use in semistructured interviews with people working in Catholic and Jesuit schools, colleges, and universities. We also invited people who work in other Catholic contexts involving youth and young adults to participate. It is important to keep in mind that we were studying the sexual abuse of vulnerable people, which includes many more people than children. Seminarians, graduate students, college students, junior faculty, and employees are all adults who may be in a vulnerable position. We settled on five questions for people who work in these environments:

- How would you describe the Catholic Church (or the Society of Jesus) as an organization?
- How are disciplinary actions conducted?
- How important is reputation?
- How do employees understand patronage?

- How are individuals promoted within the Catholic Church (or the Society of Jesus)?

There were follow-up questions related to how people understood priesthood, hierarchy, etiquette concerning reporting misbehavior, and whether discipline was the same for clergy members and other employees. The research was conducted with the approval of the Institutional Review Board at Fordham University.[21]

One of the more difficult follow-up questions, because it requires some explanation, was whether people had seen evidence of isomorphic mimicry. Sociologists of organizations borrowed this term from biology to describe how organizations can take on the appearance of being something they are not.[22] An example of mimicry can be found in the diocesan review boards that review allegations of abuse of children. A 2021 audit by the Secretariat of Child and Youth Protection for the National Review Board and the U.S. Conference of Catholic Bishops indicated that 30 percent of the diocesan review boards were dysfunctional due to lack of meetings, inadequate composition or membership, not following the by-laws of the board, members not confident in their duties, lack of rotation of members, and lack of review of diocesan/eparchial policies and procedures.[23] In other words, what is said or promised in written rules is often a far cry from what is actually done.

A report from the Associated Press provided more evidence of mimicry. Their report revealed that bishops were appointing church defense attorneys and top aides to the boards.[24] Bishops also controlled whether issues went to the board, what evidence the board could see, and what criteria they must use in making decisions. Additionally, all of the work of these boards is confidential.[25] It is important to recognize that the 2021 audit indicated that 70 percent of the dioceses and eparchies had functional review boards—at least according to the standards laid out in the charter. The difference between these dioceses is the character and diligence of the individual bishops, which is a reflection of how power is personal.

We learned a great deal about mimicry over the course of this study. It seems to be endemic in the Catholic Church, though this is much less true of Catholic and Jesuit colleges and universities as well as K–12 schools than seminaries and dioceses. Colleges and universities have a great deal of third-party oversight from state and federal authorities, accrediting agencies, and grant-giving foundations. Catholic grammar and high schools are also accountable to state departments of education and local child welfare regulations. Seminaries, on the other hand, have much less oversight and enforcement of standards even though they are also accredited.

As a lay member of one of the teams in the 2006 Apostolic Visitation of American Seminaries and Houses of Formation, Anderson found two seminaries that admitted men who were not academically prepared but did not enroll them in academic programs. The seminaries did this so that these men and their records would not be shared with accrediting agencies. The *Program for Priestly Formation* (*PPF*) that governed U.S. seminaries at the time said that men should receive a master of divinity or an equivalent degree before being ordained; however, the bishop who was the chair of the team explained to Anderson that the *PPF* did not say that men must receive the degree.[26]

The *PPF* mandated that candidates for priesthood must spend four years in a seminary, but it did not require them to earn any actual degree. The chair of Anderson's team explained that bishops can dispense with anything that is prefaced with "should" or "ought." The new *PPF* says that seminaries *should* have degree programs certified by appropriate accrediting agencies and that seminarians *should not* be excused from pursuing an accredited degree except "for serious reasons."[27]

The contemporary *PPF* also reveals that even mandated impediments to admission in the seminary can be dispensed with by bishops or by the Apostolic Penitentiary for particularly grave impediments.

> The seminary is obligated to determine the freedom of the applicant from the impediments and irregularities for receiving Holy Orders and from conditions that must be addressed prior to the reception of Holy Orders, namely, that sufficient time has passed for a neophyte…that the applicant does not "labor under some form of amentia or other psychic illness"…and that he has not committed voluntary homicide, positively cooperated in a completed abortion, gravely and maliciously mutilated himself or another.…If any of these conditions exist, then prior to admission, appropriate dispensations or remedies must be obtained.[28]

We share these examples to help you imagine the danger that mimicry poses to the church's capacity to fulfill its mission if it admits seminarians who are unable to complete a degree in divinity, who suffer from serious mental illness, or who have committed homicide, and subsequently ordains them. Mimicry is not an institution or a rule, but it is a symptom of rules that result in persistent failures.

Having settled on questions that should elicit formal and informal rules, we invited a large cross-section of people who work in Jesuit and Catholic organizations from schools to seminaries as well as people who have worked in dioceses or with the United States Conference of Catholic Bishops. In the end, we found thirty-nine participants. Most participants worked in different regions of the United States though a few worked in international settings. Their age varied from their thirties to their eighties, and their collective service was over 1,100 years of experience.

We must note that this group of people who have served the Catholic Church or the Society of Jesus spoke from a place of love and concern. They all continue to serve in Catholic and Jesuit organizations. Some of the categories below overlap in that many participants have experience in multiple settings:

- Catholic priests (current and one former): 15
- Jesuits: 13
- Religious (current and two former): 17
- Non-Catholic priest: 1
- Men: 28
- Women: 11
- University/seminary experience: 31
- High school experience: 16
- National youth ministry/outreach: 5

Some interviews were held in group sessions, and others were with individuals. Because we focused on people holding leadership positions in the Catholic Church and the Society of Jesus, there were almost four times as many men who participated than women.

There was significant concern over anonymity among the participants, which we included in our Institutional Review Board Protocols. All the materials from the interviews have been made anonymous. The only identifying information is whether a participant was a Jesuit, a member of a religious order, and a general description of the position the person held. If it is relevant to the testimony and does not compromise anonymity, we also include references to gender and minority status.

Our study is not large enough for quantitative analysis, but we hope to open a path for others to extend the research and develop instruments to identify conditions that make sexual abuse more likely. We believe what we found needs to be shared broadly so that Catholics with experience in economics, political science, sociology, organizational psychology, management sciences, and other fields can bring their knowledge and experience to bear on the problems with the "humanly devised institutions" in the church. Recognizing the limitations of this study, the consistency of the responses to the questions reveals the Catholic Church is caught in what economists call a "capability trap," which siphons off an organization's capacity to function effectively and to thrive. It is a trap because it creates a form of bounded rationality that blinds people from recognizing problems or solutions or both. Because the impetus to hide the crimes and failures of priests flows from the idealization of priests and the church, our capability trap is ultimately a clericalism trap.

Disentangling ourselves from the clericalism trap requires three steps. First, we must understand how formal and informal institutions (rules) create what North calls "path-dependent" behavior in the church. We will draw on the experience of those who work to implement institutional reform in international development to explain the nature of a capability trap. Once we understand how institutions contribute to creating traps for fragile states, we need to discern how Catholic rules relate to scripture and tradition, why they emerged, and how they have been transmitted to the contemporary church.

Having explained the theoretical, theological, and historical issues, we then concentrate on what we have learned from the interviews. Rather than taking a thematic approach to describe what we found, the material is organized by the setting or context of the interviews. Next, we will present what we learned by interviewing Jesuits, which provides insight into religious communities. Our focus on the Society of Jesus results from the fact that the Jesuits supported our study to identify institutional deficiencies. Much of what we learned is likely to apply to other religious communities. Indeed, the participants who belonged to other religious orders expressed admiration for how the Society of Jesus forms its members and performs apostolic works.

The following chapter explores how clericalism and the rules it engenders manifest themselves in Catholic and Jesuit organizations, particularly those that work with children, youth, and young adults. Though we concentrated on Jesuit schools and universities, we also interviewed people who work for diocesan universities and those sponsored by different religious communities across the economic and ideological spectrum.

These chapters highlight the conditions that make sexual abuse and its concealment more likely. Not all of these conditions are overtly insidious or specifically Catholic. For example, the more a school or university seeks to have staff, faculty, and students identify with the organization, the less likely people are to report abuse.[29] The higher the reputation of a school or university, the less likely victims will report abuse.[30] Of course, we want our schools and universities to have well-earned reputations and foster a sense of belonging, which means that we need to be intentional in establishing safeguards, metrics to evaluate them, and a process for improving them. The chapter concludes by indicating the various ways that rules related to clericalism and pastoral care are stripping the church of its capacity to improve its effectiveness as an organization.

Our findings suggest that if the church is attempting to be more evangelical and attractive to people, it should begin with institutional reform and an improvement in both governance and management. Perhaps we could retrieve an appreciation of one of the guiding principles of the Council of Constance: What touches upon all must be approved by all. The Council of Constance allowed lay leaders to vote on its canons and decrees, including those that deposed three popes, so it would seem that we could create forms that keep bishops and religious superiors accountable to the people their decisions affect.

We conclude by presenting a strategy for escaping the trap; however, we avoid providing too much specificity. Institutional reform is much more likely to succeed when it includes local people's involvement because they are forced to assess existing structures' weaknesses in ways they normally do not consider. This new awareness leads people to build coalitions across networks to deal with common concerns. Rather than attempting to present a detailed solution, we are advocating for a problem-solving approach to institutional reform that is consistent with the principle of subsidiarity. We are inviting Catholics to examine these issues, on the one hand, to liberate them from an idealized understanding of the church and, on the other, to bring their gifts to bear on making our community safer and healthier.

Because we are trying to reach many people, we will be writing in as straightforward a manner as possible. We will limit technical terms, and we will keep the notes to what is necessary to explore our sources more deeply. There has been a great deal of valuable scholarship on the sexual abuse crisis in terms of ecclesiology or the theological study of the church that has considered how we understand holy orders, the idea of communal sin, and the need to incorporate the social sciences into our analysis of the problem. Nonetheless, as Neil Ormerod has recently written, "In general the engagement with social sciences by ecclesiologists has been eclectic, sporadic, intermittent, and secondary to what they (theologians) view as their primary task."[31]

Though we are not going to engage in the methods used in other social sciences, which would result in long digressions into methodological concerns, we hope this book will encourage the practitioners of the social sciences to apply their disciplines to sexual abuse in the Catholic Church, since we know that sexual abuse arises from its human rather than the divine dimension. We will concentrate on the institutions or rules, but they are related to organizational structures. *Structures*, in the sense we deploy the term, refer to administrative or governance systems, apparatuses, and mechanisms such as offices, departments, processes, committees, and synods. We will offer some suggestions in terms of structural reforms, but we believe that there are experts in political science, public policy, and corporate governance who can refine our suggestions or envision more effective structural changes while avoiding the problem of mimicry.

Although we are writing about holy orders and the ordained, we primarily have priests and bishops in mind. We are not excluding the deacons, who can also suffer from clericalism. Permanent deacons are also ordained, but they have not been idealized in the same way as priests. Deacons have not been identified with the structures of the church either. Part of this is due to the fact that historically the permanent diaconate was subordinated to the priesthood and came to be seen as a transitional order. It was not until 1967 that the church reestablished the permanent diaconate. Perhaps the permanent deacons, who have not been idealized, can help provide a healthier model of ordained ministry—one that does not base its legitimacy on claims of perfection but on humble service.[32]

CHAPTER 2

IDENTIFYING THE TRAP

Clericalism is a trap. This is true whether you consider it an ideology or a sin. The early church frequently described sin in terms of lures, snares, and pits, which are all various forms of traps leading to bondage. Ideology, which can be seen as a value-neutral term in the social sciences, has negative connotations in Catholic theology. Pope Francis warned about the temptation to make the gospel an ideology, which he portrayed in terms of reductionism.[1] Further, there is a popular tendency to contrast truth with ideology across the Catholic spectrum. Ideology in economics is a neutral term, but not all ideologies are equal. Some are productive, and others are counterproductive.

Ideologies in the sense we are using the term are simply models, theories, and beliefs that have been colored by "normative views of how the world should be organized." Ideologies shape the formal and informal institutions—the rules of the game as we discussed in chapter 1—providing incentives and disincentives to the choices we make. The rules alter the price people pay for acting on their convictions. They assure cooperation by clarifying when punishment is required and by providing incentives to enforce them.[2]

The idealization of the priest and of the church has created a host of perverse incentives to hide sin and failures on the part of the clergy. Hiding problems makes it virtually impossible to diagnose their causes or to envision appropriate remedies. To use Douglass North's language, the church is stuck on an unproductive path. He explained that organizations become path dependent when a set of rules initially provides a benefit, though they create disincentives for further development or improvement.[3]

When formal and informal rules provide a short-term benefit but limit growth, members of a society or organization develop a stake in maintaining them. Those who benefit from the rules will generate an ideology to rationalize the society's structures and to account for its poor performance.[4] Because these formal and informal rules develop gradually and incrementally, history matters when considering how to implement effective and sustainable institutional reform. The task is more complicated when it comes to the Catholic Church because it requires sorting whether the claims of papal apologists, canon lawyers, theologians, popes, and councils are authentic articulations of apostolic tradition or manifestations of the social and political demands of their historical context. Such adaptations to changing circumstances can be well thought out and reasonable or poorly considered and destructive, but in either case, they are provisional.

DISCERNING BETWEEN WHAT CAN CHANGE AND WHAT CANNOT

How can we discern between what are infallible traditions and what are humanly devised ideologies or institutional rules? In other words, how can we distinguish between what can change and what cannot? This question has been at the forefront of theological treatments of the church since the Modernist crisis in the early twentieth century and has become a point of division in the Catholic Church. Rather than attempt to settle such a contentious question, we will simply employ the guidelines set forth by the first decree of the Council of Trent:

> The council clearly perceives that this truth [of salvation] and rule [of conduct] are contained in written books and in unwritten traditions which were received by the apostles from the mouth of Christ himself, or else have come down to us, handed on as it were from the apostles themselves at the inspiration of the holy Spirit. Following the example of the orthodox fathers the council accepts and venerates with a like feeling of piety and reverence all of the books of both the

> old and new Testament, since the one God is author of both, as well as the traditions concerning both faith and conduct, as either directly spoken by Christ or dictated by the holy Spirit, which have been preserved in unbroken sequence in the Catholic Church.[5]

This passage has the status of extraordinary magisterium, which means that the Catholic Church officially recognizes it as infallible because it is a doctrinal definition by an ecumenical council.

To explain the significance of Trent's statement on traditions, we need to briefly outline what is known as the "notes of authority" and the discussions that led to this definition. There are varying systems of notes that Catholic theologians who were called "manualists" devised to distinguish the different levels of authority of different teachings. While the manuals they created are interesting, none of these elaborations are definitive; however, there is a general consensus among ecclesial theologians that there are three levels of authority to magisterial teaching or official church teaching: universal ordinary magisterium, extraordinary magisterium, and ordinary magisterium.

Perhaps the least contentious category is the extraordinary magisterium of the Catholic Church. It consists of matters pertaining to faith and morals that the Catholic Church has defined as infallible or irreformable doctrine by ecumenical councils or popes. It includes all the definitions of faith, including the creeds, Christology (two wills and two energies), *Theotokos*, the veneration and use of icons, transubstantiation, seven sacraments, the statement on scripture and tradition, justification (including original sin and baptism), papal infallibility, immaculate conception, and the assumption of Mary. The final two are the only doctrines defined by a pope. While this list is not comprehensive, it represents the bulk of the doctrines the church has defined as infallible. Before promulgating a definition, councils and popes have to show the doctrine's roots in scripture or the apostolic tradition.

Most of the contemporary disputes over authority and change involve ordinary magisterium and universal ordinary magisterium. Universal ordinary magisterium is recognized as infallible and unchanging tradition because it is what the Catholic Church has always taught—meaning since the time of the apostles. As a category, it holds all of the defined and undefined infallible truths. It is the indeterminacy of universal ordinary magisterium that opens the door to controversy. An example of this is when John Paul II declared the teaching "that priestly ordination is to be reserved to men alone has been preserved by the constant and universal Tradition of the Church" before concluding "that the Church has no authority whatsoever to confer priestly ordination on women."[6] His use of the word *teaching* is important because he claims that this is not a practice or a discipline, which could be changed. As pope, he could have defined the teaching, which would have been an act of extraordinary magisterium, but he chose not to. This means he was using *ordinary magisterium* to claim something is universal ordinary magisterium.

Ordinary magisterium refers to the teachings of bishops, councils, and popes that have not been defined as infallible. There is an extraordinary range of the types of teaching in this category, from the pronouncements of a local bishop at the lower level to a papal encyclical or a pastoral constitution originating from an ecumenical council at the higher levels of authority. Ordinary magisterium is provisional in the sense that it can be appropriate for certain historical circumstances, but it requires revision in light of new contexts and developments in our understanding of the world. It can also be wrong.

The list of examples of erroneous teaching by the ordinary magisterium is long and includes many scandals. As John Henry Newman noted, the majority of the bishops supported the Arian heresy at various points in the trinitarian controversies of the early church.[7] Newman wrote that in the fourth century "the divine tradition committed to the infallible church was proclaimed and maintained far more by the faithful than the episcopate."[8] Ordinary magisterium provoked the witch hunts of the fifteenth century, the suppression of scientists like Galileo, and supported slavery in many places around the world. Even so, there is an effort to present the ordinary magisterium as perfect by denying that it ever promoted immoral positions.

A good example of the inability to admit magisterial error is the 2023 Vatican statement from the Dicasteries for Culture and Education and for Promoting Integral Human Development on the "doctrine of discovery." The doctrine of discovery justified the oppression and slavery of Indigenous people. The idea was promoted by Pope Nicholas V in the bull *Dum Diversas* (1452), which gave the king of Portugal the right to invade and subdue Muslim and pagan countries and to reduce their people to slavery. Nicholas reaffirmed his position three years later in the bull *Romanus Pontifex* (1455) and added that the pope had the apostolic authority to dispose of the whole world. Almost forty years later, Pope

Alexander VI released the bull *Inter Caetera* (1493) that legitimated the Spanish conquest of the "New World."

The Vatican dicasteries were unable to admit that the ordinary magisterium in the fifteenth century was wrong. Their statement shifts what was clearly presented as doctrine at the time to simply being matters of political expediency:

> The "doctrine of discovery" is not part of the teaching of the Catholic Church. Historical research clearly demonstrates that the papal documents in question, written in a specific historical period and linked to political questions, have never been considered expressions of the Catholic faith. At the same time, the Church acknowledges that these papal bulls did not adequately reflect the equal dignity and rights of indigenous peoples. The Church is also aware that the contents of these documents were manipulated for political purposes by competing colonial powers in order to justify immoral acts against indigenous peoples that were carried out, at times, without opposition from ecclesiastical authorities.[9]

The statement makes it sound as if these papal bulls just emerged out of historical circumstances rather than being authored by men with objectives that were contrary to the mission of the church. Moreover, people in the fifteenth century did see these papal bulls as expressions of the Catholic faith. Why not admit that these popes, bishops, priests, and lay leaders were mistaken?

Disputes arise when people attempt to claim some ordinary teaching is, in fact, part of the universal ordinary magisterium. Some of the ordinary magisterium is what the church has always taught and thus can be included as universal teaching; however, when theologians and bishops identify current teaching as universal ordinary magisterium, they are more often than not simply deploying an apologetic strategy to foreclose communal discussion and discernment. We do not seek to define what the church has left undefined because every definition leads to division rather than unity. To define means to draw a line between who is inside and who is out. Such lines can be necessary, but they should be drawn with reluctance because the mission is to include as many people as possible in the work of manifesting the kingdom of God. This is why we use the existing definition from Trent of what can be changed and what is permanent.

Even when one begins with a defined doctrine, understanding the historical context is important for interpreting it.[10] One of the problems that faced the Catholic Church during the Reformation was that it had no definition of what was or was not an infallible tradition. Some theologians included as infallible traditions canon law, the writings of the saints, all statements from ecumenical councils, and papal decretals. Traditions also included the Mass, sacraments, and liturgical practices. The problem was that statements from these various sources frequently contradicted one another or were no longer practiced.

Protestant objections to the authority of the church and of her traditions were fairly consistent and unanimous but Catholic answers were not. It was urgent to unify theology on this matter. To do so, the bishops at Trent distinguished between the authority of apostolic and postapostolic traditions. They determined that only apostolic traditions are infallible. This led to an objection because in apostolic traditions, several matters of discipline were known to have been canceled such as facing the East for prayer or standing at Mass during Lent. Since the church had changed liturgical and ceremonial traditions from the apostolic era, they determined that they could not be irreformable traditions.[11]

After significant debate, the Tridentine fathers determined the apostolic traditions that have infallible authority are limited to those treating matters of faith and morals. With its stress on apostolicity, the decision made it impossible to hold that new infallible doctrines may be revealed to the church. Obviously, there can be and must be new doctrine on most matters. Doctrine is simply what the church teaches, some of which changes as we learn more and as our context changes. For something to be infallible or irreformable—to meet the test of tradition—in the sense of being binding on Roman Catholics, a doctrine must be an apostolic tradition on faith and morals. While a definition of a doctrine can come later than the apostolic era, such as the doctrine of the Trinity, it has to be grounded in the apostolic tradition. Trent provides us with a tool to distinguish between what can change and what cannot; or to put it another way, it presents a dividing line between what is humanly devised and what is divinely inspired.

Many humanly inspired institutions or rules are positive adaptations to historical circumstances; however, all of the deficient rules, such as concealing the crimes of the clergy, lie on the human side of the equation even if they are promulgated by a pope or an ecumenical council. Using Trent's definition as our dividing line, we are opening up a wide vista as to what could be changed. Such discernment is necessary if we want to combat the idealization of the priesthood and of the church, which rests on deep but nonapostolic foundations.

ORDINATION, OFFICE, AND ORGANIZATION

Clericalism, the idealization of the priest, has blurred the distinctions between ordination and office as well as between office and the organization. This poses a problem for understanding the dynamics between formal and informal rules driving decisions because institutional analysis employs distinctions between organizations and their institutions, organizations and their members, and organizations and their objectives.[12]

Economists had routinely assumed that members and organizations shared the same objectives when they constructed their models, but this assumption limited their ability to predict performance. Douglass North wrote,

> One cannot make sense out of the world with just economic reasoning. You have to know political and social theory and, as you are going to see, you must also know some cognitive science. Now, the reason why of course you need all these is that we do not live only in an economic world, a political world or a social world; we live in a world that is a blended mixture of all these. In the world that we are trying to confront with respect to solving problems, we have to develop a body of theory that integrates all of them.[13]

To solve real problems, we must account for the diverse objectives of priests, which requires distinguishing between who they are as a person and the office they hold. The New Testament advises us to look for false teachers and pseudo-prophets in the church who "have eyes full of adultery" and "hearts trained in greed" (2 Pet 2:14). Scripture warns Catholics that some teachers or leaders in the church do not share the mission to be a "sacrament or instrumental sign of intimate union with God and of the unity of all humanity."[14]

Economists generally use sports analogies to explain this distinction between an organization's objectives and those of its members. The objective of a baseball team, for example, is to win games; however, an individual or group of players might have other objectives that are inconsistent with winning. Players might deliberately throw a game for their personal financial gain, which is what happened in the 1919 Black Sox scandal. Blurring the distinctions between the members and the organization provides cover for members whose objectives contradict the organization's mission. They also obscure how institutional rules and the incentives they establish affect behavior. Rather than recognizing institutional or structural problems driving behavior, people shift responsibility to individuals—the proverbial "few bad apples."[15]

This blurring of the distinction between a man and his office creates a type of perception filter where people ignore, minimize, and explain away behaviors that are inconsistent with the office of the bishop or pastor. This is one of the reasons that person-focused approaches to solving problems, like those employed in pastoral care, are less effective at solving sexual abuse. The Australian Royal Commission described some of the difficulties as arising from the fact that perpetrators seek to conceal their activities and many of the behavioral indicators of abuse or grooming are ambiguous, which requires interpretation to decide if they are concerning behaviors.[16]

When people have to interpret ambiguous information, they employ heuristics—rules of thumb—to produce conclusions quickly. Heuristics generally have a high degree of accuracy in everyday circumstances, like quickly recognizing someone in a crowd, but they also can lead to persistent biases in decision-making.[17] There are two biases that are particularly relevant to the sexual abuse scandal. The first error arises from the representativeness heuristic: We assess people on their similarity to the standard for other people in their group.[18] The second is confirmation bias: We tend to notice evidence that confirms our initial opinion of someone and to interpret ambiguous evidence in a way that supports our bias.[19] Since most people who are ordained ministers or members of religious orders are caring and loving people, the default position is to think well of them, which is reinforced by confirmation bias.

Institutions or rules also have a heuristic function, and some amplify the representative and confirmation biases, as seen in the infamous case of Cardinal Theodore McCarrick. McCarrick made a positive and durable first impression on Pope John Paul II. When the pope learned that McCarrick was known to have shared his bed with young men in the bishop's residence in two different dioceses and with seminarians at a beach house, he reached out to four New Jersey bishops to confirm whether the allegations were true. The bishops confirmed that

McCarrick liked to share his bed with young men, but they "did not indicate with certainty that McCarrick had engaged in any sexual conduct."[20] Of course, there is no way they could know with certainty that he was having sex with the men in his bedroom without being present. Rather than strip McCarrick of his position as a bishop for sleeping with seminarians in the privacy of his bedroom, John Paul II decided to move him to Washington, DC, and make him a cardinal archbishop.

While we may be falling into hindsight error—overestimating how obvious a situation should have been—John Paul II should have known better. It was not a question of whether McCarrick had young men share his bed because he admitted to it; however, he denied that there was any sexual conduct and blamed those allegations on politically motivated gossip. The report states, "Though there is no direct evidence, it appears likely from the information obtained that John Paul II's past experience in Poland regarding the use of spurious allegations against bishops to degrade the standing of the Church played a role in his willingness to believe McCarrick's denials."[21] As we shall see, there are rules going back to at least the Fourth Lateran Council (1215) to privilege the testimony of highly placed clergymen over their accusers.

Contemporary magisterial documents blur the distinctions between officeholders and their offices in ways that make it difficult to imagine bishops behaving like McCarrick. While progressive Catholics like to point to the ways that Vatican II advocated for more agency on the part of the laity, it also preserved and transmitted clericalism. *Lumen Gentium* states that bishops are "heralds of faith" and "authentic teachers of the apostolic faith." It does not say that they *should be* "authentic teachers." The Second Vatican obliges Catholics to follow the bishop "as Jesus Christ follows the Father." In this way, Catholics are taught to assume that bishops share the same objectives as the church, which obscures the possibility that they are acting from selfish motives. This idealization of the bishops generates rules requiring deference to their testimony and their decisions. All of these statements are emphasized and diffused throughout the global church by means of *The Catechism of the Catholic Church*.[22]

The ultimate expression of the blurring of distinctions between the person and the office is expressed in terms of an ontological change effected at ordination. Although it is possible there are appropriate ways of defining *ordination* in terms of ontological change, the imprecision of this language has generated a theology of priesthood that is impious at best, as can be seen in this statement, which is posted on the Vatican website, from Cardinal John O'Connor:

> In my judgment, this concept of the ontological nature of the priesthood, is critical. We don't just put on vestments; we don't just receive an assignment. Neither makes us priests. We become priests at ordination. There is an "ontological change" in our spiritual nature. Such is a profound mystery. Is it too bold an analogy to compare the change to Christ the Son of God's retaining His Divinity while becoming a man? Or to observe that after bread becomes the Sacred Body of Christ, it still tastes like bread and feels like bread, but is now the Body of Christ? There has been an ontological change. A cup of wine still smells like wine and tastes like it, but it is now the Blood of Christ. At ordination an ontological change takes place.[23]

Since priests already share a human nature with Christ, it begs the question of what their transubstantiated nature is. While this idea is apparently supported by the Vatican's webmaster and Cardinal O'Connor, it has no support in apostolic tradition. In fact, no one wrote about ordination effecting some sort of ontological change prior to the Second Vatican.

As Robert Swanson pointed out, there is no firm biblical basis for the concept of ordination and it does not appear in Isidore of Seville's list of sacraments, which was composed prior to 636. It took almost six hundred more years before holy orders became one of the seven generally accepted sacraments. Moreover, medieval churchmen drew a distinction between the inalienable character of ordination and the exercise of its powers, which could be permanently suspended. There was not even consensus that ordination entailed an indelible mark, as can be seen in the rites to degrade criminal clerics before they were turned over to the secular authorities for punishment. Swanson notes that one text even used the term *exordination*: "The fact that a translated bishop did not need to be reconsecrated, yet lost jurisdictional authority over his former diocese and had to acquire it over the new one, shows a distinction between the power of orders and jurisdiction which could be applied to an ex-bishop."[24]

Our point is that ordination was not equivalent to office. In the Middle Ages, a priest or bishop who was ordained but was not installed into a position had no right to any form of jurisdiction or to perform the sacraments except in rare and emergency circumstances. Though we have a different sense of offices than medieval Christians, priests and bishops continue to be dismissed from the clerical state, as can be seen from Canon 292: "A cleric who loses the clerical state according to the norm of law loses with it the rights proper to the clerical state.... By the loss of the clerical state, he is deprived of all offices, functions, and any delegated power."[25] Yet the idealization of the priesthood communicated through magisterial documents identifies the cleric with his office, functions, and power. Blurring these distinctions has affected how power is understood and practiced.

Governance overreach is another casualty. While apostolic tradition supports the idea that pastors have a role in governance, it does not specify how that governance is carried out. Even a passing knowledge of church history indicates that governance has been understood and practiced differently over time. For example, we know that in the apostolic era the local community elected bishops. Over time, governance shifted to an imperial model as part of the Roman Empire, then to a more feudal form of government in the early Middle Ages, and finally adopted a monarchial model in the late Middle Ages that largely remains in place. These adaptations of governance to changing historical and cultural circumstances demonstrate that the Catholic Church can move beyond its monarchial model.

As Richard R. Gaillardetz noted in *Ecclesiology for a Global Church*, the New Testament presents the formal structures of ministry relationally. Ministry in the apostolic era was understood as a call to public communal service and had little relationship to the notion of office that would emerge later.[26] Insofar as the Gospels describe how governance should be carried out, they offer little more than this injunction from Mark 10:42–45:

> So Jesus called them [the apostles] and said to them, "You know that among the Gentiles those whom they recognize as their rulers lord it over them, and their great ones are tyrants over them. But it is not so among you; but whoever wishes to become great among you must be your servant, and whoever wishes to be first among you must be slave of all. For the Son of man came not to be served but to serve, and to give his life as a ransom for many."

Unfortunately, this quite clear directive has not been implemented as a rule that has become normative, routine, and unconscious. On the contrary, there was a deliberate effort by popes, bishops, and priests to claim the authority to rule over others.

Resistance to the emergence of the monarchial church developed almost immediately. St. Bernard of Clairvaux (1090–1153), a Cistercian abbot and doctor of the church, was one of many who argued that popes and bishops could not claim apostolic rights to things the apostles did not have. The Apostle Peter was responsible for the churches, but Bernard emphasized that he did not possess wealth or dominion. He asked Pope Eugenius III (r. 1145–1153) to listen to the words of 1 Peter 5:3: "Not in lording it over your charge but making yourself a pattern for the flock." Since Christ absolutely forbade the apostles from acting like the kings of the nations and lording it over the people, Bernard concluded, "It is clear: dominion is forbidden for Apostles."[27] In short, the saint was reminding Pope Eugenius that magisterial authority is not equivalent to monarchial or imperial power.

According to St. Bernard, the power of the apostles was the power of the keys or the power to exclude sinners from the sacraments.[28] The other forms of jurisdiction and power held by popes and bishops are not apostolic, which means they are conditional and can be subject to limitations as well as oversight.[29] His arguments reflect St. Peter Damian's position that God takes power away from the bishops who fail to discipline their priests when they commit crimes.[30] For Peter Damian, another doctor of the church, God uses the laity to strip the clergy of the power that the laity granted to them. Wealth and power are not apostolic rights. Even if the apostles had other forms of power beyond the exclusion of public sinners from receiving the sacraments, they bear little resemblance to the extensive and self-referential claims of power on the part of our contemporary bishops. Our goal is not so much to outline how the church ought to be governed as to demonstrate that there is much that could be and needs to be changed in order to escape the dynamics of path-dependent behavior.

ELEMENTS OF THE CLERICALISM TRAP

Given the dynamics between formal and informal institutions, there is a broad consensus in economics that institutional embeddedness requires third-party enforcement of reforms until they become customary and normative.[31] Such enforcement requires clear metrics for performance and specific remedies for the officeholders or authorities who fail to meet them. These measures are required to break away from path dependency, which economists have described in terms of a capability trap. A capability trap robs an organization's capacity to implement reform and move forward. Clericalism, the idealization of the priests, is an ideology that reveals the Catholic Church to be closer to a fragile state than a perfect society.[32]

As we saw in the introduction, "isomorphic mimicry" describes how organizations can take on the appearance of being something they are not.[33] Organizations that have been given tasks that they cannot perform are tempted to adopt mimicry as a strategy to deflect criticism.[34] In terms of states, it describes situations where it is simpler to create what looks like an organization with ranks, offices, and policies than to create a functioning organization. This can be seen in organizations like the police in fragile states where there are ranks of officers, but they do not actually serve the purpose of protecting the people and providing justice.

Mimicry becomes an optimal strategy when an organization exists in an environment in which the space for innovation is closed, there is no functional evaluation of performance, and the organization holds a monopoly position.[35] Most Catholics would recognize that the Catholic Church is not known for creating space for innovation and we found that there is no functional evaluation of performance when it comes to leadership in the Catholic Church, but could we say that the Catholic Church holds a monopoly position? Perhaps it is better to say that the church is a quasi-monopoly. There are other churches and religions, but if you believe the teaching of the magisterium in documents such as *Dominus Iesus*, the Catholic Church is necessary for salvation.[36] Even those who reject the Catholic Church's exclusivist doctrines face disincentives to exit the Catholic Church such as alienating family members and damaging social relationships. While such concerns have diminished over the last fifty years in the United States and Europe, they remain stronger among Catholics in the Global South. Given these conditions, mimicry is an attractive strategy to deflect criticism over scandals from the laity.

Mimics, whether they are in the Catholic Church or in fragile states, take on the appearance of capable organizations following "best practices" but lack a drive or even metrics for performance.[37] Insofar as the Catholic mimics frame their objectives in terms of pastoral ministry—defined in terms of personal power—they claim that their work and performance cannot be measured objectively. Under these conditions, an organization can thrive simply by projecting an appearance of being functional regardless of the outcomes and the behavior of its front-line agents.[38] A good example of this dynamic can be seen in Pope Francis's *Vos Estis*, which charges the metropolitan bishops with investigating their suffragan bishops without establishing any metrics to evaluate their performance or consequences for failure. Establishing organizations without a metric for performance naturally flows into the second element of the capability trap, wishful thinking.

The dangers of wishful thinking have to do with unrealistic expectations over how quickly reforms can be implemented. It fails to recognize the limitations regarding organizational capacity and the ease with which it can be established. Organizational capacity is how economists describe whether an organization has the personnel, training, and resources to accomplish initiatives at various scales.[39] Catholics tend to think in terms of universal implementation even when they are aware that the church is made up of people who belong to different cultures with diverse political, social, educational, and economic contexts. The capacity of dioceses in the United States varies widely as well. The Diocese of Savannah, Georgia, does not have the capacity of the Archdiocese of Chicago, Illinois.

Wishful thinking can be manifested in many ways, but a common form of this tendency is the identification of a reform champion or group of champions in powerful positions who will implement change.[40] Blaming the leaders suggests that corruption results from individual failures rather than systemic or institutional deficiencies, which would mean that the right approach is to call leaders to conversion. Attempting to implement institutional change through leaders fails to recognize that powerful leaders in formal positions are the most embedded in their institutional context and are the least likely to perceive the need for change.[41] Another weakness of relying on leaders to implement institutional reform is that members with lower positions in an organization have internalized institutional rules and are unlikely to change simply because leaders command them to do so.[42]

Even when there is some progress in implementing reform, the failure to meet the expectations engendered by wishful thinking erodes legitimacy and trust, which are also part of an organization's capacity to act. In this way, wishful thinking leads to premature load bearing. Premature load bearing refers to situations when an organization is expected to move forward so quickly that it actually makes things worse.[43] Economists use the analogy of an athlete who begins to compete too quickly after an injury and exacerbates it further. Organizations succumb to this when they are asked to do "too much of too little too soon too often."[44] When an organization adopts policies or laws without the ability to implement them, it creates parallel universes between the law or public policies (*de jure*) and the real characteristics within it (*de facto*).[45] As a result, they further erode the capacity to function thereby reinforcing the tendency to embrace mimicry. While mimetic strategies can help an organization survive in the face of public criticism, they do so by further sacrificing integrity and functional capacity.[46]

How does this apply to the church? *Vos Estis* is paradigmatic. There are many positive elements such as its calls for transparency, third-party reporting to church authorities, involvement of laity, and a process for metropolitan bishops to exercise oversight. However, it entrusts the bishops to police themselves, has no role for the laity in assuring the law is being followed, and lacks an enforcement mechanism.[47] Many metropolitans will make a good faith effort to implement the provisions of the document in an effective manner, but they lack the training, the staff, and the resources to implement the new law. Moreover, history should lead us to expect that a few metropolitans will not embrace the new law or will find reasons or strategies to avoid applying it rigorously. Worse, the law may be unevenly applied because it runs contrary to the implicit rules of patrimonial patronage and fraternal relations among bishops.

Even though *Vos Estis* represents a step in the right direction, it is wishful thinking that Pope Francis can promulgate a new law and solve the problem of sexual abuse. If all of the metropolitans miraculously decide to do their utmost to implement a law contrary to the received rules of the game, they do not have the capacity to do so and some of their efforts will fail. The failures will be an indication of premature load bearing. Even though the failures may be limited to a small number of cases, they will undercut the credibility of the church further with ever larger numbers of people. To borrow a phrase, what happens in the Archdiocese of Las Vegas, will not stay in Vegas. This is true of every diocese, and it is true of the provinces of the religious orders. Given the church has staked its credibility and authority on the holiness of priests and bishops, there will be a strong motivation to hide failures.

More than a motivation, there is a tradition of hiding failures, not an apostolic tradition but a tradition nonetheless. The rule that people should hide clerical failures emerged after the papacy of Gregory VII. Rules related to silence have deep roots in the apologetics over ecclesial liberty or the independence of the clerical establishment from lay oversight. As we shall see in the next chapter, the idealization of the priests began as part of the polemics between popes and secular rulers over power and influence took on a quasi-dogmatic quality. People like Jan Hus would be burned at the stake for publicizing the sins of the clergy to the laity in the early fifteenth century. The idealization itself, insofar as it claims almost ontological power differentials, serves as a disincentive to report abuse and other crimes. To strip clericalism of its power, we must understand its origins and transmission to us. Once you see how clericalism emerged and observe its corrosive effects, the self-perpetuating institutions or rules that clericalism generated become clear.

CHAPTER 3

A HISTORY OF CLERICALISM

Arguments over who has authority are as old as the church itself. St. Paul asserted his authority as a spiritual person to respond to divisions in the Corinthian community in 1 Corinthians 2:15: "The spiritual person judges all things and is himself judged by no one."[1] This verse has a long and complicated history. The monks identified themselves as spiritual men, as can be seen in the writings of John Cassian (d. 435). Monks used 1 Corinthians 2:15 to claim their authority to settle theological disputes and to assert their independence from episcopal oversight. By the early twelfth century, diocesan clergy began to appropriate this passage to themselves as they engaged in a series of struggles with monastic priests over who had the right to exercise pastoral care.

There had also been struggles between the popes and emperors in the early church, but they were not framed in terms of an idealized priesthood. Pope Gelasius (r. 492–496) argued that Christian emperors could not define Christian principles: "There are essentially two powers governing the world: the sacred authority of pontiffs and the power of kings."[2] Shortly after Gelasius's papacy, a dispute between an Arian Gothic king and Pope Symmachus (r. 498–514) resulted in the creation of a document that historians call the Symmachian Forgeries, which state, "The first see shall not be judged by anyone."[3] However, the Forgeries were advancing the claim that the Bishop of Rome could not be judged by a council of bishops. This principle was included in another forgery, the Pseudo-Isidorian Decretals, and made its way into canon law, where it remains today as Canon 1404.[4]

The Pseudo-Isidorian Decretals, which were written sometime between 845 and 851, aimed at providing total immunity to Frankish bishops from imperial prosecution.[5] The forger was almost certainly responding to the way Emperor Louis the Pious retaliated against the Frankish episcopate after a rebellion in 830.[6] The Pseudo-Isidorian Decretals appealed to St. Paul's teaching that the spiritual person judges all things but is judged by no one, but the author did not link this principle to holiness or perfection. This forged text was not well received prior to the second half of the eleventh century, when a new apologetic for the power and independence of the clergy began to emerge. This new apologetic argued for ecclesial power on two fronts: the perfection of holy orders and the inherent dignity of providing pastoral care.

These efforts to promote the liberty of the church by elevating the clergy above even the most highly placed lay leaders coalesced in the papacy of Gregory VII (r. 1073–1085) and gained momentum in the succeeding centuries. Pope Gregory VII used ideal models of priests to exhort and admonish the bishops to reform themselves and their priests. Over time, the ideal portraits of priests were severed from the corresponding warnings to "Judas priests," leaving an idealized understanding of the priest in ways that made it difficult to distinguish between the ordained man, his office, and the church itself.[7] As the Catholic bishops became more invested in the rhetoric of perfection, they became increasingly alarmed by the prospect of scandal. In order to keep priestly crimes over sexual matters quiet, they promoted a pastoral response to priests and bishops accused of crimes and tried to ensure that clergy were tried in church and not civil courts.

MEDIEVAL APOLOGETICS AND PATH DEPENDENCY

John O'Malley, SJ, has called the Gregorian Reform a landmark event in the history of the church and has designated it "a great reformation" in that the reformers gradually replaced rules consistent with feudal society concerning who had the right to install men into benefices.[8] It also replaced the rules as to who had the right to discipline and correct the clergy. The apologetic for the liberty of the church crafted by

Gregory VII and the later "Gregorian reformers" denied that the clergy should be subject to secular laws, that the church should pay taxes, and that the laity could publicly criticize the clergy. These issues were deeply contested by royal apologists, monks, mendicants, and theologians from the eleventh to the sixteenth centuries; nonetheless, after some initial setbacks, the Gregorian reformers won significant victories that established path dependency.

The medieval controversy over who had the right to invest a man into a benefice had significant economic implications. The benefice system was established by Charlemagne and supported by his heirs to provide a means of support for the clergy and religious as well as to provide charitable works on behalf of the poor. Those who were installed into a benefice were entitled to a portion of the revenues generated by the church, diocese, or abbey in which they served. Colin Morris has illustrated how, over time, both the lords who held the rights to the benefices and the clergy installed into them began to see churches, abbeys, and dioceses as revenue sources that could be leased in the same way as a mill or a toll bridge. As a result, the benefice system nearly erased the model of the church as a community of believers by the middle of the eleventh century.[9]

Both ecclesiastical and secular leaders who held the right to install men into these benefices frequently sold the positions to raise revenues or to consolidate their power in some other way. Buying and selling benefices had been condemned as the heresy of simony, but the practice continued because it was firmly ensconced in custom as an informal institution. Pastoral care reformers opposed simony because it led to the installation of untrained and mercenary men who were not committed to a life of virtue into ecclesiastical offices. Unfortunately, Rome did not have the capacity to enforce the laws against simony.[10]

By restricting who had the right of investiture, Gregory VII hoped to limit the number of unworthy ecclesiastical officeholders undermining the quality of pastoral care. He developed an apologetic for ecclesiastical liberty based on the dignity of the pastoral office and the need to improve the quality of the men installed into those roles. The pope was not opposed to investiture or the benefice system; instead, he aimed at transferring investiture rights held by the laity to the papacy and episcopacy, which he promoted as a restitution movement.[11] While the pope faced resistance to implementing this institutional change, the promise of ecclesial liberty and the transfer of investiture rights provided powerful incentives for subsequent popes, bishops, and other prelates to support his agenda.

Rather than starting from personal holiness or service to justify ecclesial authority, Gregory VII argued for the superiority of sacramental power to royal power. He asked whether male members of the nobility could create the body and blood of the Lord by their word to illustrate the superiority of priestly power.[12] Gregory went so far as to claim that exorcists, who were unordained members of the clergy, were superior in power and dignity to kings because they commanded spirits rather than men.[13]

Gregory exhorted prelates, a term that primarily refers to bishops but includes other leaders in the church, to measure themselves and their subordinates in terms of the pastoral care models of holy priests transmitted by Gregory the Great and others. By leaving it to the prelates to measure themselves and the clerics under their rule with exhortatory and thus idealized models, Gregory VII's policies unintentionally opened an enormous degree of latitude in church discipline. This distinction between the holiness of the individual cleric and the dignity of the clerical order built upon an earlier distinction Peter Damian had used to respond to rigorist reformers of his day. The rigorists claimed the sacraments of prelates guilty of simony were invalid.[14] Peter Damian believed that all clergy guilty of simony should be deposed; however, he realized that denying the validity of their sacramental acts was inconsistent with the mission of pastoral care. In short, the rigorists' position implied that sacramental power was rooted in the person rather than the sacramental office, which would mean that people were indebted to men rather than to God for their salvation. Peter Damian argued,

> There is one, indeed, who prays but another who hears the prayer; the one who asks, differs from him who approves the petitions. What man dares to compare himself to Peter and John? And yet it was said of them that they went to Samaria to impose hands on those who had been baptized, they prayed for them and they received the Holy Spirit.[15]

He concluded that the Samarian ordinations were not valid due to the personal gifts of Peter and John but resulted from the Holy Spirit's response to their prayers. Peter Damian's goal was to reassure people that the church could provide for the care of souls regardless of the purity or impurity of its ministers; however, Gregory VII reframed this distinction to emphasize the inherent dignity of the priestly office.

The emphasis Gregory VII placed on priestly dignity was designed to deny lay investiture rights as well as the right of lay leaders to assess whether priests lived up to the demands of their office. He strictly reserved this role for the clerical hierarchy, drawing upon the patriarchal assumptions of medieval society to justify his position:

> Who may doubt that the priests of Christ are to be reckoned the fathers and masters of kings, princes, and all of the faithful? Is it not acknowledged to be a sign of wretched insanity, if a son should try to subject to himself a father or a disciple a master, and to make subject to his power by wrongful obligations him by whom he believes that he can be bound and loosed not only on earth but also in heaven?[16]

Bernold of Constance, a contemporary, exhibits how his ideas were received when he wrote, "He [Gregory VII] wished that the ecclesiastical *ordo* should not be in the hands of laymen, but rather should rise above them by virtue of the holiness of their conduct and the dignity of their *ordo*."[17] Gregory VII wove strands of pastoral theology, patriarchy, and an idealized model of priesthood together into a cord that could not be broken easily.

Other contemporaries, such as Emperor Henry IV, were less enthusiastic than Bernold. The emperor drove Gregory VII out of Rome and placed his own man on the papal throne. Even so, subsequent popes who carried his agenda forward won important victories with the Concordat of Worms (1122) and the Golden Bull of Eger (1213). With the Concordat of Worms, the emperor ceded the right to invest men in ecclesiastical offices, though he could still invest them in secular offices. Almost a century later, Emperor Frederick II conceded the free right of appeal in all ecclesiastical matters to Rome, traditional rights to the personal property of deceased bishops, and the revenues generated by vacant sees in Germany. Following the Concordat of Worms, Gregory VII's theology was quickly incorporated into twelfth-century sources such as Gratian's *Decretum* as well as into influential works of theology such as Hugh of St. Victor's *De Sacramentis Christianae Fidei*, which is the first *summa* in theology.[18]

The process whereby Gregory VII's apologetic began to take on a quasi-dogmatic quality fits the pattern of how organizations develop path dependency. His justification for the liberty of the church had reaped considerable economic and political benefits to the papacy and the episcopacy, but it undercut the Catholic Church's capacity to implement sustainable reforms. Medieval popes simply did not have enough personnel or power to enforce the canons consistently and uniformly. The repeated promulgation of canons against lay investiture, simony, and clerical concubinage at councils held in 1123, 1139, 1179, and 1215 reveal that the problems persisted. Even though there were some successes, reform tended to die with the prelates who supported it, and the existing rules, formal and informal, reasserted themselves.

FOURTH LATERAN COUNCIL (1215) AND ITS CONSEQUENCES

The Fourth Lateran Council advocated for pastoral care reform and the liberty of the church from secular oversight. Preaching to the assembled bishops at the council, Pope Innocent III advanced the cause of ecclesial liberty by elevating the authority of the papacy to include complete jurisdiction over the entire church—including the secular rulers. He distinguished the authority of the pope from that of the other bishops and the lords:

> Yet, who am I, or what is my father's house, that I may be seated more eminently than kings, and occupy the throne of glory? For to me it is said in the Prophet [Jeremiah], "I have constituted you over nations and kingdoms, that you may root up and destroy, lay waste and scatter, and that you may build and plant" [Jer 1:10]. To me also it is said as to the Apostle [Peter], "To you I will give the keys to the kingdom of heaven, and whatever you bind on earth will be bound also in heaven; and whatever you loose on earth, will be loosed also in heaven" (Matt 16:19). When he [Jesus] spoke to all the apostles, he said in particular, "Whose sins you forgive, they are forgiven them, and whose sins you retain, they are retained" [John 20:23]: When, on the other hand, he spoke to Peter alone, he said universally, "Whatever you bind on earth will be bound also in heaven; and whatever you loose on earth will be loosed also in heaven"

> [Matt 16:19]; because Peter can bind the others, but he cannot be bound by others.[19]

His understanding of papal primacy was codified in Canon 5 of the Fourth Lateran Council, which stated that the "Roman Church has a primacy of ordinary power over all other churches."[20] Pope Innocent III famously continued by pointing out that Peter alone received the fullness of power and that as the Vicar of Christ, he was less than God but greater than a human being.[21]

Pope Innocent knew that the sins and crimes of the priests were undermining the credibility and authority of the Catholic Church. The church was struggling to respond to challenges posed by the Cathars, who were dualists, and the Waldensians, who were free preachers. Because both groups pointed to the impurity of the Catholic clergy, Pope Innocent III declared,

> When heretics see us sin, they teach that our preaching should not be listened to, proving this by the authority of Sacred Scripture, which says, "God said to the sinner, 'Why do you expound my laws and put my covenant in your mouth [Ps 50:16]?'" When an offensive mediator is sent to intercede, the animosity of the angry plaintiff is provoked to worse things, because if his life is despised, it follows that his preaching is held in contempt, and it may be said to him, "Physician, heal yourself;"...The prophet also, before he is commissioned to preach, is first cleansed of sin, and his mouth is touched with a coal taken from the altar with tongs.[22]

According to Innocent, this purity was necessary for the priest to be of service to the people.[23]

Purity or pollution rules function to uphold the value of an institution or to reinforce social identity.[24] For example, the *Decretum* called priests to fast longer and more than laypeople prior to Easter. The rationale was to uphold the value of priesthood and to promote priestly identity. Just as the lives of clerics ought to be different from those of laypeople, the canon states, so too there should be a distinction in the way they fast.[25] Gratian concluded that even though these ordinances were enacted, they were never approved by common use, so they had the force of exhortation rather than law; otherwise, those who did not follow these canons would have to be deprived of their rank because clerics who disobey the canons immediately forfeit any office they hold.[26] Gratian did not consider the question of how such a disobedient priest might be identified and publicly removed from office.

Clerical superiority and independence rested on the cultic holiness of priests and the dignity or perfection of the clerical *ordo*, which created incentives to mimicry and to hide clerical crimes.[27] They also led to the development of formal institutions that created disincentives to reporting. The effort to conceal clerical malfeasance can be seen in the Fourth Lateran's Canons Seven and Eight. Canon Seven directed prelates to prudently and diligently correct their clergy. The bishop was advised to correct by ecclesiastical censure as the care of souls requires, which positioned Canon Seven in a pastoral rather than a judicial framework. Canon Eight outlined the process prelates should employ for investigating and punishing clerical crimes and instructed superiors to investigate when some outcry or rumor reached him, but only after determining that the rumor or accusation did not come from malevolent or slanderous people. Further, investigations should only begin if the matters come up more than once.

Since the council fathers at the Fourth Lateran assumed many people make false accusations against prelates, Canon Eight instructed superiors leading investigations to avoid acting as an accuser or as a judge. It warned that accusations against priests threaten the stability of the church and affirmed that accusations against them should not be admitted readily. The only time a criminal complaint that could result in a priest losing his status could go forward was "when his offenses are so notorious that it cannot be ignored without scandal or tolerated without danger." Even in such notorious cases, the council mandated that superiors should act out of charity when deciding on how to punish the offenders.[28] If such a complaint against a powerful prelate was allowed to proceed, the Canon declared that the accused must be provided the depositions with the witnesses' names attached, which created a strong disincentive to make accusations.[29] In effect, the process established by the Fourth Lateran was a form of mimicry.

The council appeared to create a legal process for investigating and punishing the clergy, but it served to discourage accusations, investigations, and loss of status due to offenses such as simony and clerical sexual sins. Insofar as it identified the prelates with the columns of the church, it reveals the lack of distinction between the organization and its agents.[30] It formalized the rule that the testimony of superiors was more reliable than that of subordinates. Given that all members of the clergy were deemed superior to the laity, the process made it difficult and dangerous for the laity to make an accusation. What appeared to be a disciplinary process was in fact a pastoral care process for clergy that was guided by charity rather than justice for priestly offenders. But the effect was to make clergy a privileged class.

The Fourth Lateran also passed Canon 46 forbidding the taxation of the church by secular authorities without papal consent, which led to the controversy between Boniface VIII (r. 1294–1303) and Phillip of France (r. 1285–1314) over ecclesial authority and independence.[31] Phillip had taxed the church to raise money for his war with Edward I of England (r. 1274–1307). In response, Boniface VIII issued a papal bull threatening to excommunicate rulers who taxed the church without his consent. His argument rested on an idealized understanding of clergy that had been formulated by Giles of Rome (1247–1316). Giles wrote,

> Perfection or sanctity or spirituality is of two kinds: the one is personal, the other according to status. Thus the status of the clergy is more perfect than the status of laity, and that of rulers than that of subjects; but if we speak of personal perfection, there are many laity who are holier and more spiritual than clerics, and many subjects who are more so than rulers....But if we speak of perfection or spirituality according to status, and especially according to the status of prelates, which consists in jurisdiction and fullness of power, then he who occupies the holier and higher status will judge more things and will not be able to be judged by his inferiors; for as the Apostle says at I Corinthians 4, "He who judges me is the Lord."[32]

In the case of the pope, he argued that since the pope holds the holiest status, it is fitting, reasonable, and probable that he was personally holy as well. Citing Gregory VII, Giles concluded that the Roman See "either receives a saint or makes a saint."[33] By doing so, he effectively erased the distinction between personal and positional holiness. Boniface VIII incorporated Giles's premises into *Unam Sanctam* and concluded that "it is altogether necessary to salvation for every human being to be subject to the Roman Pontiff."[34]

CLERICALISM AND THE GREAT WESTERN SCHISM

As the crisis in the papacy deepened with the Great Western Schism, when there were two and eventually three competing popes from 1378–1417, reform efforts coalesced behind the rallying cry *reformatio in capite et in membris* (reformation in the head and the members). Christopher Bellitto has argued the efforts at reforming the head and the members arose out of rising expectations for the church.[35] Different reformers in the late Middle Ages emphasized reform of the head or reform of the members, but they generally saw these ideas as linked. As Gerhard Ladner has shown, the idea of reform was almost exclusively understood as personal in the early and medieval church.[36] His students, Louis B. Pascoe, SJ, and Philip H. Stump, showed that reform continued to be largely conceived of in personal terms.[37] The emphasis on personal conversion is understandable given the increasing tendency to conflate office and person in the schools of theology at the time, but from the perspective of institutional analysis this idea that having a personally reformed pope who would be able to reform the members looks like wishful thinking.[38]

The blurring of distinctions between the men and the offices they held shaped how reformers understood their task. John Olin offered this description of Catholic reform:

> The state of the clergy loomed large in Catholic reform. If their ignorance, corruption, or neglect had been responsible for the troubles that befell the Church, as nearly everyone affirmed, then their reform required urgent attention and was the foundation and root of all renewal. This involved personal reform, that of the priests and prelates who are the instruments of the Church's mission and the ones principally charged with the *cura animarum* (care of souls or pastoral care). The reform of the faithful would follow as a consequence, but the immediate objective was institutional or pastoral.[39]

Olin identified the institution with the pastors and the organization with its agents, which is typical of the way church historians treat reform. Pastoral care reform rhetoric sought to exhort and admonish bishops either to implement new laws or to enforce existing ones.

Reformatio in capite was understandably the primary concern at the Council of Constance (1414–1418) given that it was called to end the Great Western Schism. The schism began in September of 1378 when the cardinal of Geneva led a group of French-speaking cardinals to defect from Pope Urban VI (r. 1378–1389). The cardinals took up residence in Avignon and elected the Genevan cardinal as Pope Clement VII (r. 1378–1394). Because the secular rulers were almost evenly divided in their support for each pope, there was no clear way to resolve the spectacle of two popes. Even the saints at the time were divided, with Catherine of Siena supporting the Roman pope and Vincent Ferrer supporting the Avignon pope.

This situation lasted for thirty-one years and had a corrosive effect on ecclesial discipline and the authority of the papacy. When it became clear that neither pope would resign and that a war would not resolve the issue without devasting Europe, people began to advocate for a conciliar solution. One of the theologians in the Conciliarist movement was Jean Gerson (1363–1429), a leading voices in crafting a justification for removing a pope from office. Since the pastoral objective of the church is the establishment of peace and unity, which he described in the Pauline terms of building up the body, he claimed it must be the primary duty of the papacy.[40]

Gerson reasoned that provisions in canon law giving the pope prerogatives against being judged by anyone cannot legitimately obstruct the need to end the papal schism. Since the church was perfectly instituted by Christ, he argued the church must have the capacity to heal itself. Citing Isaiah 1:9, he associated the idea of the remnant of God's faithful with the makeup of a council because it represents the entire ecclesiastical hierarchy.[41] Although canon law did not have provisions for calling a council without a pope or for a council to judge a pope, Gerson portrayed this as the result of the fact that canon law is a mix of all three forms of law: natural, divine, and positive. He argued that positive law is imperfect because it is written to address particular circumstances and cannot anticipate every possible eventuality.

Divine law and natural law, which aim at love, peace, and unity, are unchanging and absolute. Gerson concluded that positive law, in this case canon law, must yield to divine and natural law.[42] Because positive law frequently encounters exceptions, one must turn to the principle of equity (*epikeia*) in order to interpret the law, as the apostles did in

Acts 5:27–30 when Peter explained to the high priest that he must obey God rather than a human being.[43] Gerson's justification for ignoring provisions in canon law concerning papal prerogatives was laden with the possibility of creating other forms of accountability to divine and natural law, but he carefully crafted his argument within the confines of a papal schism or a heretical pope.

The situation worsened in 1409 when a group of cardinals used Gerson's reasoning to call the Council of Pisa (1409) and to depose the rival popes. The Council of Pisa elected Pope Alexander V (r. 1409–1410) to resolve the papal schism. This is known as the Pisan Papacy. This was an attempt to end the schism, but Alexander died ten months after being elected. Cardinal Baldassare Cossa, who had a reputation for lusting after power, was elected Pope John XXIII (r. 1409–1415) by the cardinals associated with Pisa. Given the reputation of John XXIII, many of the secular rulers who had committed to supporting Alexander reconsidered their positions and abandoned the Pisan Papacy. Meanwhile, neither the Roman nor the Avignon pope accepted Pisa's legitimacy and simply ignored its actions.

Five years later, the Conciliarists were successful at convoking the Council of Constance (1414–1418) to resolve the schism and reform the church. On March 30, 1415, the Council of Constance issued *Haec Sancta*: "First, that this synod, legitimately assembled in the holy Spirit, constituting a general council, representing the catholic church militant, has power immediately from Christ, and that everyone of whatever state or dignity, even papal, is bound to obey it in those matters that pertain to the faith and the eradication of said schism."[44] Like most medieval conciliar statements, *Haec Sancta* lacked any specific enforcement mechanism; but unlike most medieval councils, Constance had voting representation for the lay leaders of the European nations. What made this decree enforceable at Constance was the third-party support of civil authorities, particularly the emperor and the French king.

The council fathers sought to change how the church was governed. They envisioned regular councils to ensure the popes followed through on Constance's decrees against exemptions, dispensations, simony, and the ostentatious dress of the clergy among other matters.[45] The council enacted *Frequens* in October of 1417, which declared,

> For this reason (neglect of councils fosters evils in the church) we establish, enact, decree and ordain, by a perpetual edict, that general councils shall be held henceforth in the following

way. The first shall follow in five years immediately after the end of this council, the second in seven years immediately after the end of the next council, and thereafter they are to be held every ten years for ever.[46]

Obviously, this edict was not implemented forever.

The hope was that the pope, as the head, would sponsor reform of the members and that *Frequens* would ensure that reforms would continue to be spread, implemented, and policed. *Frequens* was simply ignored because there was little incentive on the part of the popes to call councils that might seek to limit papal power; furthermore, the bishops had no incentive to advocate for councils that would bring their transgressions to light.[47]

Constance set important precedents even though it failed to change the rules regarding how the church is governed. Based on the principle that "what touches all must be approved by all," Constance allowed representatives of the laity and religious to vote on its decrees. It also deposed three popes, showing that ecumenical councils can, under certain circumstances, correct popes using the principle of equity. Finally, it made it clear that canon law is distinct from natural and divine law in that it is not absolute and must be changed to meet evolving circumstances.

The Council of Basel-Ferrara-Florence (1431–1445) repeated many of the themes of Constance and tried to assert its authority over the pope on the basis of *Haec Sancta*; however, this effort failed. Over time, the support of the secular rulers eroded because Basel was challenging a pope who was duly elected and universally acknowledged.[48] Many of the council fathers, including the leaders of the reform movement, defected because they distrusted the motives of the majority that only saw reform in terms of the head, not of the body.[49] Perhaps most importantly, Pope Eugenius offered secular authorities far-reaching privileges, including the rights to benefices and the investiture of Naples, in return for their support.[50]

The result was no movement to reform, and its decrees against simony, concubinage, and other clerical excesses had little impact. The lower clergy would not accept any change to their rights and customs without a council, but the popes were unwilling to call a council for the next sixty-three years. The governance of the church would remain an absolute monarchy, but a weak monarchy that could not enforce canon law. When the Fifth Lateran Council was called in 1512, it renewed canons against a familiar set of clerical abuses and called for the conversion of the clergy.

The repeated efforts to pass or renew canons against clerical abuses were ineffective for several reasons. First, the Catholic Church did not have the organizational capacity to enforce the canons in a consistent way. Second, the council members did not understand the incentives driving behavior, particularly those arising from informal institutions such as unwritten traditions or the client-patron system. Unsurprisingly, the bishops, cardinals, and popes who led these councils did nothing that would challenge their authority to dispense with many aspects of canon law or that would diminish their revenues.

The repeated failures of pastoral care reformers in the late Middle Ages to make gains against simony, plural benefices, and other abuses through enacting new laws or processes have the hallmarks of a capability trap. The *de jure* reforms passed by the councils had little effect *de facto* on the behavior of those in holy orders. Studying the history of reform in the Middle Ages is like watching children trying to reinforce a sandcastle as the tide relentlessly comes in and erodes its foundations to the point of collapse. Pastoral care reformers would ameliorate problems, but without addressing the need for institutional reform ecclesial inertia eroded their gains.

The initial successes of the Gregorian Reform agenda stalled the capacity for institutional change by denying any role for the laity in holding the clergy accountable. Since the justification for this liberty was that the clergy were holier than the laity, at least according to their state, there were strong incentives to hide clerical crimes. The councils in the late Middle Ages took on the character of mimics insofar as they appeared to have the function of governance without metrics to evaluate compliance or functional structures to ensure accountability.

The effort to project an image of holiness became increasingly difficult with the advent of the printing press, which made it possible to publicize clerical corruption. Using the new technology Martin Luther instigated a religious revolution that led to a series of devastating wars between Catholics and Protestants. In an effort to end a civil war in the Holy Roman Empire, Emperor Charles V and representatives of the Schmalkaldic League signed the Peace of Augsburg, which set in place the principle of *cuius regio, eius religio*. As a result, the Catholic Church was able to maintain its monopoly position in much of Europe—leaving mimicry an effective strategy throughout the modern period.

After the Peace of Augsburg, the idealization of the priesthood and the rules necessary to preserve it, such as concealing clerical offenses, flowed into the present through various channels. Following the Protestant Reformation, Cesare Baronius (1538–1607) wrote a history that eradicated all evidence of ecclesial scandal and became the standard source for history textbooks employed in the seminaries until the first half of the twentieth century. Pope Gregory XVI (r. 1831–1846), whose knowledge of church history was informed at least indirectly by Baronius, declared that the church cannot need reform because it is impervious to defects of any kind.[51] Ecclesial claims to perfection were also promoted in Pope Pius IX's 1863 *Syllabus Errorum* and Pope Pius X's 1910 *Sacrorum Antistitum*.[52] The blurring of the distinction between a person and his office or between the ordained and the Catholic Church was so successful that it has influenced how more contemporary Catholic and Protestant church historians understand ecclesial reform. "Institutional reform" and "hierarchical reform" are used synonymously and interchangeably by church historians.[53]

Contemporary magisterial documents also blur the distinctions between officeholders and their offices. The primary source that communicates these ideas to the clergy and laity alike is *The Catechism of the Catholic Church*, which describes ecclesial ministry as personal:

> Finally, it belongs to the sacramental nature of ecclesial ministry that it have a personal character. Although Christ's ministers act in communion with one another, they also always act in a personal way. Each one is called personally: "You, follow me" (John 21:22) in order to be a personal witness within the common mission, to bear personal responsibility before him who gives the mission, acting "in his person" and for other persons.[54]

If ministry is personal rather than functional, then there can be no clear metrics for the evaluation of performance. The *Catechism* further obscures the possibility of assessment by citing *Lumen Gentium*'s statements that declare bishops are "endowed with the authority of Christ."[55] It does not consider the possibility that some bishops, like former Cardinal Theodore McCarrick, might be "lovers of pleasure rather than lovers of God, holding to the outward appearance of godliness but denying its power" (2 Tim 3:4–5).

In fact, the *Catechism* states that the church is the "spotless spouse endowed with holiness."[56] In this way, Catholics are taught to assume that bishops share the same objectives as the church, which generates rules requiring deference to their decisions. There is a brief mention in the *Catechism* that the church has real but imperfect holiness, however, the imperfection is located in the members rather than the church.[57]

The idealization of the clergy was useful in advocating for the liberty of the church but at the cost of honestly recognizing ecclesial deficiencies. The effort to project an image of perfection has sapped the Catholic Church of the capacity to even recognize the need for change much less implement it if it requires accountability to the laity. Cardinal Donald Wuerl provided a window into the problem of an idealized understanding of the church when he argued against employing a political model of transparency and accountability "for a reality that transcends human political institutions."[58] In this way, Cardinal Wuerl pointed to the ideology that rationalizes the Catholic Church's formal and informal institutions and accounts for its poor performance. As a transcendent reality, the church cannot be assessed by mundane standards such as transparency or be held accountable to its members. Wuerl effectively rejected *Lumen Gentium*'s teaching that the church is "one complex reality which coalesces from a divine and a human element."[59]

FORMAL RULES IN CANON LAW AIMED AT PRESERVING THE IDEALIZATION OF THE CLERGY

Given the ways that the holiness of the clergy and of the church have been promoted in magisterial teachings over the last four hundred years to support the liberty of the church, canon law reflected these teachings and continued to promote clericalism and conceal the crimes and abuses of priests. The 1917 Code of Canon Law states, "Clerics shall in all cases, whether contentious or criminal, be brought before an ecclesiastical judge, unless it has been legitimately required otherwise in certain places."[60]

The reference to legitimate requirements in certain places points to concordats, which were legal agreements, between the Vatican and nation-states. Many of these agreements granted some form of clerical immunity, but the 1917 Code maintained clerical immunity, the liberty of the church, as the norm. In those cases where the concordats required clergy to submit to civil power, canonists like Stanislaus Woywod presented it as the result of "unbelief and disregard for sound principles."[61] According to Woywod's commentary, the church allowed her clergy "to suffer indignities at the hands of the state" as a necessary concession for the church to exercise its most essential rights in ecclesial affairs.[62]

The 1917 Code forbade countries that did not have concordats, like the United States, from exercising jurisdiction over priests. This provision had no force with the predominately Protestant jurists, so it aimed at influencing Catholic judges by threatening them with excommunication for ruling against priests or bishops in civil or criminal cases.[63] It also mandated automatic excommunication for political leaders who issued laws contrary to the liberty of the church. Moreover, it prescribed punishments for any Catholic who dared to ignore Canon 120 by dragging any cleric before a secular judge by filing a civil or criminal complaint without obtaining permission from their bishop.[64]

If Catholics took recourse to the ecclesiastical courts, they entered into a system designed to conceal clerical crimes. When it came to the sexual misconduct of priests, the 1917 Code created strong disincentives to reporting. For example, it gave the victims of solicitation for sex by a priest in confession only one month to report the crime. If someone had the temerity to make such a report, the 1917 Code threatened:

> Whoever personally or through others falsely denounces to superiors a confessor of the crime of solicitation by that fact incurs excommunication resolved specifically to the Apostolic See, from which case he cannot be absolved until the false denunciation is retracted formally and the damages that might have flowed therefrom are repaired to the best of one's ability and grave and long-lasting penances are also imposed.[65]

This meant that victims needed significant proof of solicitation of sex, which would have been hard to produce without audio recordings or witnesses who had the standing to be believed.

To ensure total silence over incidents of priests soliciting sex in confessions, Pope Pius XI approved a secret document titled *Instructio de Modo Procendi in Causis Sollicitacionis* (*Instructio*), which was held in the secret archives of the curia. In this case, the curia refers to the bishop's chancery. Every diocese was required to have secret archives by the 1917 Code.

The *Instructio* dictated that the promoter of justice (the prosecutor), the defender (the defense attorney), and the judges must all be priests. Everyone involved in these cases including the victims, who are referred to as either accusers or denouncers, had to take an oath of secrecy.[66] Like the Fourth Lateran, the *Instructio* calls for a searching investigation of the accusers (victims) concerning their lives, morals, and public reputation. It instructs the promoter of justice to ask any witnesses whether the one denouncing (the victim) *is capable of lying* and whether "there has ever been any case of hatred, grudge, or reason for enmity between the one denouncing and the one denounced."[67]

Whereas victims faced excommunication and grave penances if they were not believed, priests who were found guilty were to be suspended from the celebration of Mass and from hearing confessions. In less serious cases, the *Instructio* recommends transferring the offender in order to avoid scandal. In the more serious cases of solicitation, the priest could be disqualified from hearing confession permanently.[68]

The penalty for priests who had sex with minors was to be suspended and deprived of every office, but offenders could be degraded from the priesthood only in the worst cases.[69] The *Instructio* defined the worst cases as "when, all things considered, it appears evident that the Defendant, in the depth of his malice, has, in his abuse of the sacred ministry, with grave scandal to the faithful and harm to souls, attained such a degree of temerity and habitude, that there seems to be no hope, humanly speaking, or almost no hope, of his amendment."[70] In short, the offender had to be given multiple opportunities to abuse people in order to ascertain that there was no hope for conversion.

The Royal Commission identified this as the canonical basis for taking a pastoral approach to clergy sex crimes.[71] We should note the Australian Catholic Bishops Conference response: "There is no obligation in canon law to attempt a 'pastoral approach' before commencing a canonical action relating to the sexual abuse of a child or young person." While technically true, the bishops' response failed to recognize the process set in place by the *Instructio* was a rule or institution. It holds a middle place between formal and informal institutions because it was written but was not published. Even though it was not formalized in canon law, it was disseminated to every diocese in the world. Moreover, this rule is not part of some distant history.

The provisions of the *Instructio* were reissued by Pope John XXIII in 1962 as *Crimen Sollicitationes* (*Crimen*) and extended to the religious orders. Contemporary Catholic apologists have argued that this document had little effect as it was not published and is not mentioned in the canonical literature; however, Cardinal Francis George of Chicago said in court testimony that the document was taught to him in seminary.[72] Thomas Doyle reported that he found a number of documents in cases involving accused clerics that reflected the provision of *Crimen* but that it would be difficult to determine how often it was used; nonetheless, Doyle maintained that *Crimen* was used until the 1983 revision of canon law.[73]

The 1983 Code did not expressly endorse the liberty of the church, but it continued to promote secrecy as a paramount concern. It continued to support the tradition of providing pastoral care to clerical sex offenders and insisted bishops try to cure priests before putting them on trial. Kieran Tapsell noted, "It imposed a high 'imputability' test for dismissal so that a paedophile priest could avoid dismissal simply by his being diagnosed a paedophile."[74] It also established a five-year limitation for victims to bring their cases forward.[75]

In 2001, Pope John Paul II put in place new procedures with his *motu propio*, *Sacramentorum Sanctitatis Tutela*. He increased the statute of limitations from five years to ten years from the age of eighteen. He also placed all such cases under the pontifical secret with no exceptions for reporting child sexual abuse to the police.[76] The United Nations Committee on the Rights of the Child and the Committee against Torture asked the Holy See to abolish the pontifical secret in matters of child sexual abuse and to mandate reporting under canon law. Pope Francis refused to do so on September 26, 2014.[77]

As we have seen, *Vos Estis Lux Mundi* is framed in the pastoral language of a fully ecclesial "process of conversion."[78] Many have praised Pope Francis for abolishing papal secrecy in cases of sexual misconduct by the clergy in 2019; nonetheless, Article 2 of *Vos Estis* states that all information is to be protected and treated in such a way as to guarantee its safety, integrity, and confidentiality. Article 19 calls for compliance with state laws that mandate reporting, but there are many nations and territories or states within nations that do not mandate reporting child sexual abuse much less the abuse of other vulnerable people.[79]

In the states that do not mandate reporting child sexual abuse, these crimes remain confidential and protected by the local bishop or by religious superiors. There is no mention of reporting sexual harassment or assault when the crimes involve adults. By applying institutional analysis to the Catholic Church's history, we see how formal rules aimed to preserve the reputation of priests and the church as holy by creating disincentives for reporting priests.

CONCLUSION

The idealization of priests as a means to secure clerical immunity from accountability to the laity set in place an ideology establishing insurmountable power differentials between the priests and the laity. Promoting the propaganda that the church is a perfect society or spotless bride made it less likely that people would report what happened to them due to fear of not being believed. This reputation of perfection and holiness created powerful incentives for bishops and religious superiors to keep clerical offenses secret or confidential as is evident in the canons of the Fourth Lateran, the 1917 Code, and the 1983 Code. The secrecy or, if you prefer, confidentiality surrounding accusations and their outcomes also served as a disincentive to report sexual abuse. People are much less likely to report sexual abuse if they have no sense of how other accusations were handled.

The canons and other directives concerning secrecy were not just laws. These ecclesial laws were and are institutions in the way that economists use the term. They were used routinely over centuries and are so deeply embedded that even *Vos Estis Lux Mundi* tries to preserve them wherever possible. As Joshua McElwee reported, Pope Francis still maintained the principle that the laity cannot have a role in the oversight of priests and bishops:

> Francis said the proposals, which included the creation of a new commission including laypeople to review allegations of abuse against the bishops were "too much" like those that can be expected from a non-profit organization and "neglected" the spiritual dimension of fighting the evil of sexual abuse. "The church is not a Congregationalist church," said Francis. "It is a Catholic Church, where the bishop must take on the responsibility, like a pastor."[80]

In this way, Francis made it clear he believes this is a spiritual problem that requires the primacy of a pastoral approach.

Pope Francis effectively cut off the church's deepest reserve of talent, energy, and resources to address institutional problems by categorically forbidding the laity any means to hold the priests and bishops accountable. He was perpetuating the rules that created the clericalism trap, but these rules were inculcated into Pope Francis's thinking from his experience of growing up in the Catholic Church, his Catholic education, his Jesuit formation, and his experience in leadership as a Jesuit, a bishop, a pope. Perhaps most distressing is that his position rests on a foundation we know to be composed of forgeries and lies that originated in the sixth century and later. Having traced how the idealization of the priest became quasi-dogmatic and the formal rules clericalism arose historically, we turn to see the extent to which this ideology shapes the formal and informal rules perpetuating the sexual abuse crisis.

CHAPTER FOUR

HOW CLERICALISM FOSTERS ABUSE IN THE CHURCH

When we started research on the grant, we were looking for a way to identify the conditions that foster the sexual abuse of vulnerable people as well as its concealment in Catholic and Jesuit schools, colleges, and universities in terms of the rules and incentives that guide decisions. We were also interested in finding the means to implement sustainable reform, which is another way of speaking about institutional change. Institutional change in the church will only take place once new formal and informal rules become internalized, customary, and normative. Such changes take time and sustained attention, but the first step on that journey is to identify where the problems lie.

In order to identify the conditions that make sexual abuse more likely, we drew heavily upon the research of the Australian Royal Commission into Institutional Responses to Child Sexual Abuse. The Commission's final report was published in seventeen volumes, but the underlying studies and research fill thousands of pages of material and draw upon studies from across the social sciences. The Commission interviewed 8,013 persons in private and received over one thousand written accounts from people who have experienced sexual abuse as children. They reviewed allegations of sexual abuse in more than four thousand organizations, held fifty-seven public hearings, conducted thirty-five policy roundtables, and published fifty-nine research reports. Though the Commission was studying child sexual abuse in Australia, they also drew upon research done in the United States and framed their report in the broader context of organizational misconduct.[1]

There are no comparable studies in the United States on the sexual abuse committed by lay and religious employees in Catholic organizations. Nor have we seen studies on organizational responses to sexual abuse committed by lay or religious employees working for Catholic organizations. It may be that the clericalism of U.S. Catholics is so ingrained that it is obscuring our ability to see how clerical sexual abuse exists on a continuum with the abuse committed by those who serve as lay ministers, catechists, teachers, principals, coaches, professors, deans, and presidents. While we affirm the principle that leadership must be held most accountable in a public forum, we also recognize that bishops and religious superiors do not have the capacity to conceal abuse without support from the laity and religious who work in their organizations.

The Royal Commission provides valuable research on psychological care for victims/survivors, criminal justice reforms, record-keeping practices, and preemployment screening practices. The Commission also outlined recommendations to create child-safe environments that we see as positive; however, we do not believe such policies can be effective without changing the underlying rules of the game and the clericalism that supports them. It is not a question of choosing. Both better policies and institutional reform are required.

One of the reasons we found the Royal Commission's work valuable is that it looked at child sexual abuse across public, private, and religious organizations. Since we are looking at how the church functions as an organization like other human organizations, the research provided us with a point of comparison. Though we see the same conditions creating opportunities for abuse in Roman Catholic organizations as in others, there is a difference in the scale of the problem. The Commission noted,

> The largest proportion of these survivors spoke to us about child sexual abuse in Catholic institutions. We heard from 2,489 survivors about child sexual abuse in Catholic institutions, representing almost two-thirds (61.8 percent) of survivors who told us about child sexual abuse in religious institutions and more than one-third (36.2 percent) of all

> survivors we heard from in private sessions. In private sessions, we heard about child sexual abuse occurring in 964 different Catholic institutions.[2]

To put this in context, Catholics have been the largest Christian group in Australia since the 1980s (26.1 percent in 1986); nonetheless, people in Catholic organizations reported significantly more sexual abuse in proportion to their share of the population at the time (22.6 percent in 2016).[3]

Though this is a data point we take seriously, it can be interpreted in various ways. In a 2019 article in the *Journal of Child Sexual Abuse*, Faisal Rashid and Ian Barron argued that there are significant gaps in the research on the issue of clergy sexual abuse in other denominations and faiths. They identified commonalities around institutional responses to clerical sexual abuse and concluded,

> The response of clerical authorities from a variety of clerical denominations and religions toward victims appears similar in silencing victims, predominantly for institutional reputation, often resulting in support for perpetrators. The religious context and the power dynamics of religious institutions appear to have provided a space for perpetration to thrive because of the trust accorded to clerics in the society and use of threats and blame in the name of God on children by the perpetrators. Moreover, these specific characteristics of religious institutions acted as a barrier to disclosing abuse while providing unfettered access to children, and to treat CSA [child sexual abuse] as a sin rather than a crime.[4]

Given the pervasiveness of child sexual abuse historically, geographically, and socially, they advocate for seeing clergy sexual abuse as related to the history of abusive sexuality in human societies rather than linking it to any single religious faith or denomination.[5]

While Rashid and Barron are concerned with extending research into other denominations and faiths, we are concerned with diagnosing and addressing the problem of clergy sexual abuse in our own community; moreover, we are concerned with institutional responses to the sexual abuse and harassment of vulnerable people by lay and religious employees. Then there is the problem of the many lay and religious who knew about crimes, who handled the paperwork, who provided legal counsel, who participated in minimizing suspicious behavior, and who concealed crimes. Because clericalism ultimately seeks to project an idealized image of the church, it also drives the rules guiding decisions and governing disciplinary processes involving employees—both clergy and lay—in dioceses, parishes, schools, universities, retreat centers, hospitals, and youth organizations.

The Royal Commission found that perpetrators of sexual abuse in Catholic organizations included religious brothers (32 percent), priests (30 percent), laity (29 percent), and religious sisters (5 percent).[6] Its approach was to look for conditions that make sexual abuse and its concealment more likely. These conditions shape organizational culture and interact with formal and informal rules, but they are not necessarily bad. For example, all organizations with positions where adults have authority over or care for children or vulnerable adults provide opportunities for sexual abuse. Others, such as prioritizing the reputation of an organization over the welfare of a person, do not cause abuse either; however, they are not value neutral. Catholic social teaching tradition identifies prioritizing an organization over a person as immoral. We focused our research on the conditions that seem to serve as aggravating factors, like reputation, that either create perverse incentives for people in leadership positions—whether or not they are ordained—to conceal abuse in their organizations or that create barriers to reporting abuse.

AGGRAVATING FACTORS IN AUSTRALIA

Concern over reputation in Australian organizations that work with children was a primary factor that led people either to minimize suspect behavior or to conceal the sexual abuse of minors. This was true of secular as well as religious schools. It was true of religious camps and sports leagues across faith communities. An elite reputation and a sense of loyalty also incentivize other members of a school or university, staff as well as students, to respond to threats by protecting their institutional identity.[7] The Royal Commission pointed to a case involving an elite school in New South Wales where a victim/survivor reported, "I also felt that if I reported the matter, I would be betraying my school. I had a strong sense of loyalty to Knox.…Loyalty to the school was pressed as a Knox attribute."[8] They also found that some victims/survivors did not want to disclose their abuse because of their parents' sacrifices to send them to such a prestigious school.[9]

Knox was not Catholic, but many Catholic schools, colleges, and universities have become elite institutions and thus share this incentive to protect their organization's reputation. This is especially true if one considers that being elite can mean different things to different people. Being elite can point to academic excellence, but it can also point to various forms of ideological or moral purity. Private and religious schools rely on their reputation to recruit students and solicit gifts from donors.

Power differentials compound the problem by creating disincentives for victims/survivors to report sexual abuse. The imbalance of power in organizations meant that perpetrators were more likely to be believed than victims. Many schools and colleges are hierarchically structured where staff report to a single individual. In these contexts, victims may be reluctant to report abuse because they know they may not be believed or fear retribution.[10] In this way, power imbalances create barriers to investigations, reporting, and access to justice.[11]

The barriers created by power differentials are worse for members of marginalized groups like people with disabilities, people who belong to racial minorities, or people who identify as LGBTQ+. Stereotypes of marginalized people and communities create perceptions that their testimony is untrustworthy. Organizational cultures that encourage males to view homosexuality negatively make it more likely that male victims/survivors will see themselves as responsible and less likely to report abuse.[12] Workplaces that do not respect diversity and equality are also more likely to victimize employees who, in turn, are less likely to report concerns about a child's safety.[13]

As we have seen, power differentials between the clergy and the laity in the Catholic Church were established on the foundation of an idealized understanding of priesthood—what the Royal Commission specifically identified as clericalism: The "culture of clericalism led bishops and religious superiors to avoid public scandal to protect the reputation of the Catholic Church and the status of the priesthood."[14] What was different about how Australian Catholics understood reputation from other denominations and communities was that they believed priests undergo an "ontological change" at ordination differentiating them from "ordinary human beings." According to the Commission, the idea that a priest is permanently a sacred person "contributed to exaggerated levels of unregulated power and trust which perpetrators of child sexual abuse were able to exploit."[15] They found that the personalized nature of power led to limited accountability on the part of bishops and religious superiors.

The Commission concluded that the power differentials in the Catholic hierarchy are manifested and compounded by the lack of any checks and balances in church governance structures. They singled out the bishop's unitary power as holding the executive, legislative, and judicial aspects of governance as creating a "culture of deferential obedience in which poor responses to child abuse went unchallenged."[16] Though the Catholic Church is hierarchical, they also noted that dioceses and religious institutes are decentralized and effectively autonomous in governance. As a result, they recommended that the Australian Catholic Bishops Conference conduct a national review of the governance and management structures of dioceses and parishes in relation to issues of transparency, accountability, consultation, and the participation of laymen and -women.[17]

On a more granular level, the Commission identified the lack of adequate oversight of clergy and religious working in ministry as a significant factor. They noted that bishops and religious superiors have limited capacity to individually oversee the activity of priests and religious. Further, they found the "middle management" structures, such as human resource departments, were inadequate to fill the gap.[18] The lack of effective structures and processes reinforces the emphasis on the personal qualities of leaders. When there is a good pastor or bishop or religious superior, things run relatively well; however, there are no metrics to evaluate leadership and the mechanisms for removing bad leaders are unclear. Of course, there is little appetite for exposing clerical failures because the reputation of our priests and bishops has been conflated with the reputation of the church itself.

The findings of the Royal Commission suggest that the silence and secrecy in the Catholic Church make abuse more likely. This secrecy lies at the heart of the problem of sexual abuse in the church, but its cause is the effort to preserve clericalism or the idealization of the priest and the church. The lack of transparency is intended to reinforce beliefs about clerical holiness and power. Clericalism provides camouflage for perpetrators and a motive to hide scandals. Silence creates uncertainty about the consequences of reporting and sends a message to survivors that they are not likely to be believed.

There are many apparent similarities between the contexts of the Catholic Church in Australia and the United States. There is a shared language and a similar history of being marginalized communities. In both countries, Catholics largely overcame prejudices to become culturally significant and influential. The conditions that the Royal Commission identified as fostering abuse and concealment in Australian Catholic organizations seemed familiar to us.

Institutional analysis assumes that a society's or organization's rules will penetrate subsidiary organizations, but it also considers how an organization is subject to the rules of the culture or cultures within which it operates. We wanted to verify the extent to which these conditions exist in the United States and how they interact with the rules guiding decisions in our context. We began by identifying how people understand the Catholic Church as an organization before turning to how they understood ordination. We interviewed members of other religious orders as well and found a great deal of overlap in terms of the conditions that allow for abuse and the rules guiding decisions, but we did not have the resources to conduct a broader study of religious orders.

THE CATHOLIC CHURCH AS AN ORGANIZATION

Throughout our interviews, participants consistently used several terms to describe the church. Some called the church "the mystical body," "the Body of Christ," or "the pilgrim people," which is not surprising given that those we interviewed, by and large, had at the very least studied Catholic theology at a graduate level. Of course, the word *hierarchy* came up with almost every participant. The women we interviewed quickly described the church as a "male hierarchy" and people of color rounded out the description of the Catholic Church in the United States as a "white, male hierarchy." One participant with a long career training people for ministry described the impact this way: "Within a hierarchical structure you're trying to constantly read the desires of your leader, and you don't want to confront your leader either." She went on to describe "the kind of constant looking over one's shoulder" and pressure to say what the local bishop wants you to say.[19]

Religious orders are also quite hierarchical, though their leaders serve for set terms. In the Society of Jesus, for example, Jesuits who have held leadership positions are likely to be placed in new leadership positions when their terms end. One Jesuit noted the Society is "very hierarchical because of our training with *The Exercises*" but also stressed that it is an organization focused on mission.[20] The Jesuits we interviewed also tended to describe the Society as well-structured and well-connected.[21] People who work in Jesuit schools and colleges generally agreed with the assessment that the Jesuits are well organized. One faculty member described the Jesuits as less dysfunctional than diocesan organizations but also as less transparent in their decision-making.[22]

Still, the participants expressed concepts that seemed contradictory at times. For example, during an interview with leaders who work with youth and young adults, the participants described the church both as hierarchical and decentralized:

> The first word that came into my mind was messy. In the sense that, yes, when I think of the Catholic Church as an organization, I do think of a hierarchical structure. But what I also think of is the many examples of how decentralized the church can be, especially at the local level or in the context of movements...it is hierarchical and centralized and yet also functions in a way that's very decentralized.[23]

Another reported it is complicated to describe the church as an organization, especially when considering the role of religious orders, social service agencies, and parishes.[24] Their descriptions of the church as structurally hierarchical and centralized yet functioning in a decentralized manner are consistent with the findings of the Royal Commission in Australia.

The lack of centralization is manifested in the variations that the participants identified in different regions in the United States, between one diocese and the next, from one province to another, and even on the parish level within dioceses. Catholic dioceses are unequal in their administrative capacity, wealth, demographics, and infrastructure (schools, hospitals, and Catholic social service agencies). There are also significant cultural and political differences among dioceses that mirror some of the ideological divisions between rural and urban Americans or between the "red states" and "blue states"; however, Catholic sentiments do not always reflect the broader community around them. Some of the most theologically conservative dioceses are on the East Coast, and some of the most progressive dioceses are in the Southwest. Similarly, there can be considerable variations in religious orders from province to province and even within provinces from one community to the next.

Even though everyone affirmed the hierarchical nature of the Catholic Church, there were several participants who maintained it is, at the same time, a "flat" organization. Laypeople who work in youth ministry noted that there is very little possibility for promotion working in either dioceses or national Catholic organizations for the laity.[25] One professor at a diocesan university reported that although her university was hierarchical, it was easy for a professor to arrange meetings with the president of the university and even the local bishop who sponsors the university.[26]

North maintains that subsidiary organizations have the same rules, so it is not surprising that religious orders have the same rules as the church as a whole. A former religious superior described the order as "remarkably flat" explaining, "There are very few organizations this large or that are charged with so many different jobs, opportunities, ways of being that would have the CEO that close to the majority of the people."[27] In the diocesan and religious context, there are very few steps between a diocesan employee and the local bishop or between a member of the religious order and his or her provincial.[28]

The seeming dichotomies between describing the Catholic Church and religious orders as both centralized and decentralized as well as hierarchical and flat could be interpreted as a manifestation of the analogy of faith; however, we offer the more mundane explanation that these dichotomous descriptions are evidence that the bishops and religious superiors in the United States lack of administrative capacity to oversee the activities of priests and religious, not to mention those of lay employees. Like Australian Catholics, we lack adequate "middle-management" structures necessary to implement the reforms around sexual abuse in a consistent manner, and we rely, instead, on the personal quality of hierarchical leaders, whether their term is six years or a lifetime appointment as with bishops.

Even though the Catholic Church lacks the type of "middle management structures" that one would find in most public and private sector organizations, many of the lay employees we interviewed also described a tension between being a church and being a corporation or business. By way of contrast, none of the current members of religious orders spoke about the church as a business.

One woman with years of experience working in Catholic schools in different dioceses shared, "I've walked in a lot of diocesan pastoral centers, and I'm always struck by how corporate it feels."[29] A person who works with the USCCB remarked, "I would say the Catholic Church is a corporate network, at least from my vantage point as I've seen it from the national point of view."[30] Another participant with at least thirty years of diocesan experience described the church as "part church" and "part business."[31] Generally, members of this group expressed a dislike for what they perceived as the church becoming more business-like and instead preferred more of a pastoral care approach. "We tend to think in a very kind of administrative and financial focus," one of the laymen shared. "I've seen that to be often at the detriment of the work."[32]

Some of the comments that the church was acting in a more corporate fashion seem uninformed as to how corporations tend to act, which is understandable given this group of individuals had spent all or most of their careers working within the religious sector. Still, we suspect few with corporate experience would describe the Catholic Church as running as a business in a strict sense. While there are plenty of poorly managed businesses, most successful corporations have metrics, procedures, and personnel in place to exercise oversight of their operations.

When we asked questions related to corporate practices, such as having 360-degree reviews of leadership or policies requiring pastors or bishops to recuse themselves from disciplinary processes where they have a personal relationship with an employee, no one reported those practices being in place. The reality is that the Catholic Church leans into its religious mission and legal exemptions often, whether that be to justify firing employees who do not adhere to church teaching or to maintain positions of leadership that are only open to men.

The tension people feel in various settings between seeing the church as church, which they present in terms of a commitment to the mission of Christ, and seeing the church as a corporation or business reveals the extent to which the "best practices" in other organizations influence the operations of U.S. dioceses as well as Catholic and Jesuit schools and universities. To some extent, this is the result of the church attempting to comply with laws over labor issues, education, and accounting. Religious organizations also have to put in place the practices required by their insurance companies. Because the major donors tend to come from corporate backgrounds, they frequently advocate for dioceses to adopt these best practices as well.

The problem is that all of this pressure has resulted in mimicry rather than effective change. A diocese may set up a human resources department, for example, but it has a different organization with different rules for priests. The department is invariably understaffed in a diocesan context and is driven more by the decisions of either the bishop or the chancellor than by consistent policy. The situation in Catholic schools and universities is more complex, but we also heard evidence of mimicry in those contexts.

While Catholic organizations in the United States want to project an image of good governance, one educator with experience in diocesan and Jesuit schools described the governance model in terms of monarchy:

> It's almost like a kingship at the top…sometimes it feels almost like a dictatorship. Things are dictated down by bishops and there's nothing we can control. Whether it is laity [in the pews] or even as teachers in high schools or academics…it doesn't feel like sometimes you have a voice or you're asked to give a voice, but it's not really heard….Of course, I know this depends on what diocese you're in.[33]

Monarchy, however, has not been the model of good governance for quite some time.

FAILURE TO DISTINGUISH PERSON AND OFFICE

Throughout our interviews, participants noted a consistent failure to distinguish between an individual ordained person and his office within the church. For example, a bishop of a diocese is invested with a degree of authority because of the office he holds. A bishop can ordain priests and deacons. Priests, by virtue of their ordination, can consecrate the Eucharist. Those abilities are often conflated with the individual person, investing in him a respect that may not be merited. A lay participant who has twenty years of experience working for the church on the parish, school, diocesan, and national level said, "The man is looked at one way, but the man as priest has a different aura. In some ways that diminishes the human qualities, because we associate more spiritual heavenly qualities about them, as opposed to just being a man."[34]

Another participant who works in youth ministry described the failure to distinguish person and office as existing on a hierarchy. There is somewhat of a failure to distinguish in the case of deacons, more of a failure with priests, and the greatest failure to distinguish when bishops are involved. As the participant put it, "When it comes to bishops, and I work with a number of them regularly, I find there's very little distinction that they allow in their own lives for making any kind of room between the person and office."[35]

An employee from the USCCB noted that the laity ascribe a higher value to a newly ordained priest than to a lay minister with multiple degrees—including a doctorate—and more than a decade of experience working in the church.[36] The employee went on to explain that the failure to distinguish the person from the office in the case of priests makes it seem like the priest has more authority that gives priests undue influence. "But when it comes to clergy, I think there is somewhat of a melding of the office and the person," he said. This failure to distinguish between the person and his office spans all settings, including among those responsible for security on college campuses. According to one such participant, it is "pretty hard to differentiate what the man is from the office he holds."[37]

Seminary formation does not always help priests distinguish between themselves and their office. A professor who teaches theology in a seminary that primarily serves dioceses reported that even though they knew these men well, which they said is helpful for distinguishing between the ordained person and his office, they still maintained that person and office overlap:[38]

> We can never be purely just friends. There's always a responsibility, a power differential to be attended to. And that's not to say that I necessarily hold them on a pedestal in terms of my way of relation as a friend, but at the same time...you have to have a responsible awareness of boundaries because of that reality. It affects the person as a whole even if you're talking at the most basic human level.[39]

They said that distinction leads many priests to gravitate toward other priests, describing other priests as "people who are technically their equals in terms of ordination as well."[40] Such phrasing reveals the notion that those who are ordained are superior, perhaps unconsciously held even by those involved in formation at seminaries.

While the professor stressed the need for priests to have lay friends, they spoke sympathetically of the tendency to befriend those "similarly ordained." "It takes work for them to figure out how to be in right relationship with the non-ordained," the professor said. While the professor believed they had a good relationship with their priest friends, they could see how others in similar circumstances could find it challenging. "If you didn't have a really solid human foundation, particularly in terms of celibacy formation, it could get messy very easily," they said.[41]

The situation is similar in seminaries that educate and form men for religious orders, though it is subtler. A professor who works in a religious seminary said she hoped her students on the ordination track would not see themselves as "wearing separate hats or [being] separate entities."[42] She explained that one of her primary goals is to foster the integration of their ministerial identity with their identity as a person. While she saw this as one of her objectives for both future priests and lay students, she made this distinction when it came to ordained ministers: "Once you're a minister, it's 24-7. I try to help them understand how [to] integrate their ordination into who they are as a person."[43]

We will treat the Society of Jesus more fully in the following chapter, but the Jesuits we interviewed did not show any evidence of this general failure to distinguish between priests and the office they held; however, they did reveal an effort to merge the identity of their members with the Society of Jesus. In this regard, they are similar to the other religious orders. A seminary professor with experience teaching members of religious orders said,

> And then, when it comes to religious orders like the Jesuits and all the women religious or the Franciscans or any other order, I find that there's no distinction between person and belonging to the order when the formation is done really well. And that's a very positive thing in my experience because it's [about] belonging to the community, it's not the ordination, which is a very fine distinction, but it's a real distinction.[44]

Religious priests concentrate more on their religious profession than on ordination, which is not to say that do not value ordination.

The Jesuits we spoke with strongly identified with the Society of Jesus and described it as a healthy aspect of religious life. Many identified primarily with the Society and secondarily as priests. Jesuit formation was described more as belonging to the community than as a preparation for ordination because not all Jesuits are priests. The term *Jesuits* applies just as much to the Jesuit brothers and the Jesuits in formation, who are called *scholastics*. The vow to become a Jesuit and live according to the laws of the Society of Jesus comes first chronologically, a Jesuit participant noted. There is a "Jesuit way of doing things," he said, adding that "there is a real effort to integrate these values" throughout the different stages of formation.[45]

Another Jesuit who had served as a superior offered a different perspective. "Insofar as a Jesuit is healthy, there shouldn't be a lot of distance between [the person and being a Jesuit]," he said in his individual interview.[46] "With someone who has been through formation and has a strong sense of what his identity is as a Jesuit, he will see being a Jesuit as constitutive of who and what he is. And not everybody is that healthy." Later in the interview, he describes walking into a community that "feels healthy," with members that joke around and are honest with each other. "You're not going to have problems there," he said, but admitted, "there's no way to measure it."[47]

Those we interviewed had varying interpretations of what it means to be healthy regarding ordination or religious profession. That is predictable, given the size and scope of the study. Nevertheless, considering the failure to distinguish the person and the office he holds is prevalent in the Catholic Church, the discrepancy points to an acute problem. Who decides what it means to be healthy? And on what authority? In the case of the church, including within the religious orders, leaders are believed to be appointed by God. In such a context, members of the organization are disinclined to question the prevailing view of health, decreed from on high. But as history demonstrates, church leaders are not always capable of discerning what is healthy.

There are far-reaching consequences to how the church functions as a result of collapsing the distinctions between a man and his office. "In a hierarchy like ours," a professor with extensive experience working for church organizations noted, "personnel is politics." If you have a personal relationship with the clergy holding supervisory roles, you tend to be favored with opportunities.[48] A more pernicious reality undermining the church's capacity is when ordained supervisors minimize or overlook the poor performance of employees with whom they feel a personal relationship. In response, another participant said it is the clergy who ultimately decide who "gets to sit at the table" where decisions are made.[49] Since most of those men are white, they tend to choose people they feel comfortable with for leadership positions, which means there are fewer women and minorities who play even consultative roles in decision-making.

PATRONAGE AND REPUTATION

Another way of describing the personal nature of power and politics in the church is patronage, which has both internal and external dimensions for individuals and organizations. Reputation plays a role in both forms of patronage, but we found less evidence for the ways that external patronage affects disciplinary decisions. Because we were primarily looking for evidence of patrimonial client-patron chains that could, as informal institutions, undermine efforts to reform, we did not sufficiently explore the role of donors. The fact that we did not have any bishops or members of the boards of trustees participate left the role of donors largely in the shadows. In addition to cultivating donors, bishops also play the role of patrons to schools, colleges, universities, and seminaries.

Faculty and staff in school and university settings claimed donors have an outsized influence; however, only one participant had experience with development. Apparently, most development people did not see this project as something they should support. The development person worked for a school run by a religious order and spoke out of deep concern. When asked if patronage might influence a disciplinary decision involving an employee, such as a beloved coach, the development officer responded, "Yeah, in some cases the warning should have been more severe than what they received, or sometimes they were smaller things, so there was no intervention when they didn't need to be fired or anything."[50]

The development officer was clear that this did not include criminal behavior; however, it did include types of boundary violations, such as inappropriate touching. The participant warned, "I think this can happen across the board whether it's clergy or not clergy or religious, you let small things go, you don't hold them accountable, they're small things, right, it's small, it's not a big deal, and then they build and they build."[51] As we have seen, these boundary violations can be signs of grooming and should be responded to immediately and consistently. The lack of consistent discipline sends a message that some people do not have to follow policies designed to protect minors. If this type of behavior is common in our schools, which is likely given the findings of the Australian Royal Commission, then it is also likely that donors can mitigate disciplinary responses to the sexual harassment and abuse of faculty, staff, and volunteers, whether the perpetrator is lay or ordained.

Many of the people we interviewed have worked for bishops and in diocesan contexts, but they had little insight into the relationship between bishops and donors. The McCarrick report indicated how important fund-raising is for the promotion of bishops, but it did not explore how he raised money or who his donors were. Information concerning major donors is highly proprietary and limited to a small group of people. One person who had a long career working in human resources in a diocese reported that she did not think donors have the influence to direct a bishop to protect a priest from discipline when it comes to sexual abuse of children. However, she did not feel certain that internal patronage would not play a role in protecting a church employee, whether lay or ordained:

> If you're the good friend of a person who's a little higher up, it might not make any difference whether you're nice or the nastiest person to deal with. There are some untouchables, and I think we know who they are, and you have to work around that. If it's a priest who's in leadership, I think that there may be some untouchables.[52]

Internal patronage impacts who gets hired, retained, and promoted in ways that undermine the capacity of our diocesan and national structures. A person associated with the USCCB with significant diocesan experience said knowledge and experience are significantly less important in hiring decisions than having relationships with people in the organization. "Sometimes you won't even get your first interview if no one can vouch for you," he continued. "So, the relationships are really, really key."[53] We should note that this form of patronage can coexist easily with hiring and promotion policies that appear to be rigorous and equivalent to the best practices in other organizations.

Several participants noted how patronage in diocesan and national organizations reinforces racism. A layperson who works in a leadership position with a national Catholic youth organization reported,

> I find that oftentimes we gravitate to people and to things we know and so sometimes there's an unconscious patronage....We were very comfortable with who we were comfortable with. I think that this patronage can have intercultural ramifications because oftentimes we surround ourselves with people who we know we're comfortable with—often within

> our own cultural families....Well, obviously, all the people you know and feel comfortable with happen to look just like you. So, I think that there is that kind of reality of living in that patronage culture without even knowing that there are people doing it. It's that systemic kind of familiarity that I think is there and I think that [it] breeds patronage.[54]

He concluded that this unconscious patronage leads to the exclusion of people of color from participating in planning and implementing projects because "they're not in those circles of trust." Though he was very diplomatic and did not say this directly, it is clear that many of our clergy are not comfortable working with people of color or women, which limits their opportunities to advance and give voice to their concerns.

The patronage system that is in place restricts people's ability to exercise voice in the decision-making process. A USCCB employee said that the self-censorship for the sake of continued patronage is "real and devastating."[55] "Consistently I have to find a way to say the thing in a way that holds my integrity and advances the conversation," he said, "and I will hardly ever hit that bullseye."[56] In a different interview, another USCCB person reported,

> There's a lot of really layered realities of patronage and I think at some point every ministerial employee does have to make some decisions on who or what master I am going to serve today. I think sometimes it's very easy to make the decision that I'm just going to serve the master who's going to guarantee that I keep my job and make sure I'm going to be set and comfortable versus taking the risk and saying I'm going to do what I believe is right professionally, or at least you know personally, morally....If you want to stay as an employee of the church, you've got to make those decisions about what am I willing to compromise on, what am I willing to give up, and how far am I willing to push back if I want to keep my job and stay around here.[57]

The patron he is referring to is almost always a bishop or a priest the bishop has established as his delegate.

While it might be wishful thinking, most participants believed that patronage would no longer play a role in decisions related to child sexual abuse. However, there was an acknowledgment that there were many other issues where patronage continues to undermine discipline. A third person working for the USCCB in a private interview said,

> The abuse crisis caused an awareness that moved the institution towards accountability measures. It certainly did that. One of the factors I've noticed is that the patronage related to sexual abuse is in one track, but many of the other threads in the system of the church are not necessarily at that same level. Even internally systemic prejudice and racism [are] not at the level that sexual abuse is....I think there's one standard when it comes to abuse or discipline [and] in other areas, it might be a different standard. I don't know if I had a chart where I would do all the different things that we are struggling with, whether it's sexual abuse, power, finances, or racism.[58]

His account is consistent with what we found in the interviews, namely, that the publicity associated with the child sexual abuse scandal has, for the time being, diminished the role of patronage in these crimes while leaving the racism, sexism, and power imbalances that create the conditions for abuse in place. There was less awareness of the sexual abuse of adults, which may account for Cardinal McCarrick's ability to abuse his adult seminarians and priests.

A member of a religious order who teaches in a seminary indicated that patronage allows sexual abuse to take place with seminarians:

> You know you see it [patronage] in formation, for example, where it really has a lot of potential for abuse. And, the issue is not that the structure is set up in such a way that everybody is in the patronage system. It's that some participants don't understand the boundaries that are necessary. And, I've seen it with one of my closest friends in the order that I worked with closely. [He] had the kind of relationship with some of the men that Cardinal McCarrick had, and the destructiveness of that is that they felt invulnerable, there was nothing they could do that would get them kicked out of the order. And, that led to the complete incapability of anyone else to correct them or discipline them, which was not a good situation at all. But it was not, I would say, an exception.[59]

He also shared that much of the patronage among the ordained and within religious orders is hard to see because it does not revolve around money. Instead, patrons provide prestigious assignments or open career paths.

Both internal and external patronage rely heavily on reputation to function. The concern for prestige and reputation by leaders of the Catholic Church was confirmed by participants throughout the study. Some of that focus is understandable and would surely be present in other organizations. Participants noted, for example, the value universities place on having an outstanding academic reputation. Other Catholic universities want to be thought of as "orthodox." Among nondiocesan universities, concerns about orthodoxy can lead to friction with the local ordinary. At one university, for example, a scripture scholar with an orthodox view of the Bible runs into trouble because a priest in a leadership position with the local diocese takes issue with his political leanings.[60]

Reputation is also important in Catholic schools. A lay administrator at a Jesuit high school said reputation is "paramount...there's almost like a protecting the brand thing going on."[61] Participants spoke of the need to maintain a good reputation as explaining why organizational leaders do not share the reasons for an employee's termination. "The institution looks upon it as an aberration that they are ashamed of and have taken action against," according to one participant who works in youth ministry, "and yet the institution does not want to ruin the reputation [by revealing what happened]."[62]

Catholic schools, universities, and youth organizations tend to believe that a person's individual actions will reflect on their entire organization's identity. "Hell, I think it's everything," one USCCB employee said of reputation. That emphasis on reputation helps explain the high degree of secrecy that surrounds disciplinary issues, he said.[63] A good reputation is essential to satisfy the donor base.

At every level—parish, school, university, and national organization—participants noted an inclination to silence or deemphasize matters that cast the church entity in a negative light. We repeatedly heard of priests who "disappeared" from their positions without explanation. The stated intention was often "not to embarrass" the person being reassigned. However, leaders seemed less concerned with not embarrassing lay employees. That difference reveals the power differentials that exist between the clergy and the laity.

POWER DIFFERENTIALS

There was no question among lay participants that lay and ordained are treated differently by leaders in the Catholic Church and within Jesuit organizations. The question was often met with laughter because it was so obvious to those we interviewed. Said one participant, "There is an unquestionably different application of standards on how people are disciplined if you're clergy versus lay. Absolutely."[64] Another, who has experience both at the national and diocesan level, said, "At the diocesan level, from what I've seen, people are more apt to report misbehavior of other lay people than they are of clergy—unless the misbehavior of clergy has escalated to a certain level that's above what lay people would be reported for."[65] Or as another participant said, "Lay people have no security and the members of the order have complete security. It's the way things are structured."[66]

Also, for the most part, participants acknowledged regional differences in how disciplinary actions were carried out. The relationship between the ordained and laypeople requires "a level of awareness and respect for the boundaries on both sides," one participant said.[67] This power differential is further illustrated by men on the ordination track having their education paid for by the religious order or diocese, whereas with religious women or laypeople, "there is nobody sponsoring you. I mean even religious sisters. It's like we don't have the money for that or how is this going to benefit our community economically."[68] That financial question, related to education, ends up being a factor that cuts out both lay and religious sisters from governance conversations.

One participant described the difference ordained men perceive between themselves and laypeople this way: "You're in a club and these other people are not. So, I will look out for you. Because I know you. And in some respects, at times, it's like I value you more than I value them."[69] The difference between lay and ordained was further articulated by an individual working at the USCCB. With respect to lay ecclesial ministers, he said "they have no formal office as it's defined by canon law."[70] As one of the participants remarked, canon law articulates the rights of priests, bishops, and cardinals differently: "It kept talking about how no one may judge a cardinal except the pope."[71]

The remark called to mind the dispute between Archbishop José H. Gomez of Los Angeles and Cardinal Roger Mahony, the retired archbishop of the city. In 2013, the Archdiocese of Los Angeles released documents related to priests accused of sexual abuse of children. The records of fourteen of the priests were unsealed as a part of a civil case. Archbishop Gomez said in a statement,

> The behavior described in these files is terribly sad and evil. There is no excuse, no explaining away what happened to these children. The priests involved had the duty to be their spiritual fathers and they failed....We need to acknowledge that terrible failure today. We need to pray for everyone who has ever been hurt by members of the Church. And we need to continue to support the long and painful process of healing their wounds and restoring the trust that was broken.[72]

As part of the announcement, Archbishop Gomez announced Cardinal Mahony would "no longer have any administrative or public duties."[73]

Despite the controversy, months later Cardinal Mahony attended—and voted in—the conclave that elected Pope Francis. He was later appointed by Pope Francis as his special envoy in celebrating the 150th anniversary of the Diocese of Scranton, Pennsylvania. Whereas the notorious quality of Cardinal Mahony's crimes generated a public statement, he was quietly allowed to continue lower profile public duties. In this way, Pope Francis reinforced the idea that powerful members of the clergy are not held accountable and that the laity cannot rely on the pope to maintain discipline for bishops who allowed sexual predators to destroy people's lives.

SILENCE AND LACK OF TRANSPARENCY

Silence and secrecy are among the categories the Royal Commission lists as disincentives to report misbehavior. The blanket of silence is framed in pastoral terms such as charitable discretion aimed at protecting individual's reputations. Most participants, for example, described a prevailing lack of transparency when it came to disciplinary matters both in Jesuit institutions and in the Catholic Church in general. They noted a tendency for both lay and ordained employees to vanish without explanation. "You know, so all of a sudden, here today and gone tomorrow and nobody knows what happened," one professor reported.[74] Another professor described instances of disciplinary action involving priests as "hush hush" and elaborated, "If one of them randomly moved across the country or something, you knew something was going on. But they were not fired. Nor is it public."[75]

The same professor said this level of secrecy also takes place at the high school level. Once an issue had been reported, the person who made the report would rarely hear about it again. Responding to these remarks, another participant said she had encountered the same phenomenon. "Folks get ghosted away. You know what I mean?"[76] What happened never comes to light, she said. An administrator who works at a Catholic university described an incident where a student filed a complaint against a staff member and named the participant as a witness. The matter was handled privately, she said, and she never learned what happened.[77]

The point is further illustrated by a participant who works at a high school run by a religious order. She described a different standard for publicity for students and for teachers. "Even if a student says or reveals something, you have an obligation to report this and follow whatever policy says," she said. "If there's a disciplinary action between teachers, that's really kept a secret." Another said that the worse the behavior, the more likely it was to be kept secret.[78] One participant—a religious order priest from a university setting—put it this way: "The brother has a right to be protected…to have his privacy protected and it's a real responsibility to do that."[79]

Silence is instilled in priests during formation. A religious order priest said that, for example, seminarians at diocesan seminaries may be less inclined to share what was on their mind because it could result in a report to the rector. Such reports "could stop or block their ordination," he said. Knowing that possible consequence could lead to silence. Another, along similar lines, said of his order, "We don't have a kind of snitching culture."[80] On a national level, an individual from the USCCB said that disciplinary action tended to be dealt with in a secretive manner "or it respects privacy to a fault." He described the intention as "not to embarrass" the person who had misbehaved. The exception is in the case of child sexual abuse, he said, when disciplinary action is public because it must be. "When it comes to other issues of financial abuse, power abuse, employee abuse, other forms of positional abuse, we still are in the mindset of 'let's not embarrass the institution. Let's not embarrass the person.'"[81] Yet the reputation of secrecy is itself damaging, as one participant noted. "And I think the bishops' conference is a case in point. The perception and the reality of secrecy in the institution is such that it damages meaningful reputation among, you know, perhaps not among Catholics in general, but certainly among informed Catholics in a certain way."[82]

Silence is damaging to reputation, but silence also functions to discourage people from reporting sexual abuse or to identify any disciplinary matters whatsoever. Silence extends to more mundane matters such as how well a principal, dean, or president manages enrollments, retention, or academic standards. It extends to the performance of diocesan directors, leadership in Catholic social service organizations, and in Catholic media organizations. People who do not perform well are not evaluated in an open and transparent process. Reviews of performance are strictly hierarchical and confidential, which amplifies the effects of patronage and reinforces power differentials throughout Catholic organizations. Even new initiatives that have failed such as efforts at evangelization are declared a success before they are quietly shelved in order to protect the reputations of those involved. Our discomfort with examining failure prevents us from taking advantage of postmortem examinations of what went wrong or how things could be improved.

CONCLUSION

According to the people we interviewed, all of the conditions that foster sexual abuse and its concealment identified by the Royal Commission are present in the Catholic Church in the United States. The imperative to protect the reputation of the clergy and of the church is paramount and extends to subsidiary organizations such as religious orders, schools, universities, and Catholic nonprofits. In some cases, the rule to keep things silent is written into policies, but there is an overarching informal rule that we should practice "charitable discretion" when confronting the failures of the members of these organizations. Further, our participants were clear that the higher hierarchical position a person holds, the more emphasis is placed on the importance of maintaining his reputation and privacy.

The higher the hierarchical position, the more the man is identified with his position or office. United States Catholics, like their Australian counterparts, ground these power differentials in metaphysical terms of ontological change. Unfortunately, this reinforces the role of patronage so that employees, volunteers, and consultative boards are mirror images of the bishops leading our dioceses and in national Catholic organizations. In this way diverse and marginalized voices tend to be excluded from committees addressing policies, the promotion of social justice, and the development of formation programs. If members of marginalized groups are present, it tends to be in a marginal manner. As we have seen, inclusion in a patronage system requires significant self-censorship. Having a seat at the table is not equivalent to being heard.

Because power is personal, because people report to a single person, and because information is confidential, it is easier for bishops and religious superiors to conceal the crimes of the people they sponsor. The emphasis on reputation creates strong incentives to conceal scandalous behavior and is justified in terms of the pastoral aim of reconciliation. Not only is power personal, discipline is personal. When people cannot expect the consistent application of the law or policy, they are less likely to report abuse. The emphasis on personal power and the patronage system within the church is an impediment to developing robust administrative structures and the capacity to exercise oversight over the diverse operations of ordained, religious, and lay personnel. As we shall see, the rules that support the idealization of the priests and of the church penetrate subsidiary organizations, including the religious orders. There can be no solution to the perduring abuse crisis without uprooting the idealization of the priesthood, which has stripped the church of its dynamic capacity to change. No religious institution, however revered, should be spared the scrutiny that is required for the protection of vulnerable populations in our church. We need the courage, as a church, to not only identify problematic structures and rules in organizations we have come to love, but to admit how we as a community have enabled those structures to endure.

CHAPTER 5

THE EFFECTS OF CLERICALISM ON THE SOCIETY OF JESUS

Ignatius of Loyola is rightly referred to as the central founder of the Society of Jesus. While he had many early collaborators, it was Ignatius who inspired them and guided them through an early version of *The Spiritual Exercises*. Nevertheless, the first generation of Jesuits—several saints among them—from the start formed a bond of brotherhood upon which the Society of Jesus was built. Despite being separated for much time and by vast distances, this small community remained committed to each other and to the mission to save souls.[1]

In 1534, seven of these companions, including Ignatius, took vows of poverty, chastity, and obedience. They took these vows at least four years before institutionalizing their community and six years before being formally recognized by the pope. Such steps likely seemed only a formality to these first Jesuits, so thick was their brotherly love for each other. Ignatius, Peter Faber, and Francis Xavier had formed a proto-community as roommates at the University of Paris. But this community, which began as an informal band of brothers, exploded on the world stage. In 1556, the year Ignatius died, more than one thousand Jesuits ministered in Europe, Asia, Africa, and the New World.

Today, more than fifteen thousand Jesuits serve in more than a hundred countries, making the Society of Jesus the largest male religious order in the Roman Catholic Church. Their influence is felt on every continent. The Jesuits' prominence in education is exemplified by the more than 2,700 schools and universities they run, including 27 colleges and universities and dozens of schools in the United States alone.[2] From their inception, the Jesuits have been missionaries and theologians who developed a reputation for promoting social justice and human dignity. Drawing on their commitment to the Humanist idea of *eloquentia perfecta*, the Society has invested in media engagement as central to fulfilling its mission. The Jesuits list more than a hundred publications on their international website. Yet despite the size of the Society of Jesus and the diversity of its members, the Jesuits we interviewed reflected a brotherhood likely akin to that of the first companions.

The Jesuits we spoke with strongly identified with the Society of Jesus and described it as a healthy aspect of religious life. Many identified primarily with the Society and secondarily as priests. Jesuit formation was described more as belonging to the community than as a preparation for ordination, because not all Jesuits are priests. The vow to become a Jesuit and live according to the laws of the Society of Jesus comes first chronologically, a Jesuit participant noted. There is a "Jesuit way of doing things," he said, adding that "there is a real effort to integrate these values" throughout the different stages of formation.[3]

According to institutional analysis, subsidiary organizations reflect the rules of the larger organization, and the Jesuits who participated opened a window for us to see the ways that institutional rules operate in a religious order that is part of the larger Catholic Church. While commonly referred to as an *order*, in terms of canon law, the Society of Jesus is a religious institute. The distinction is an important one, according to one of the Jesuits we interviewed, who had a significant background in canon law. Canon law, he said, uses the term *institute* to emphasize that religious institutes have rules and constitutions but are in themselves "rules" or "institutes." He explained,

> We talk about a particular way of living, of a particular institute, a particular way of ministering, a particular way of proceeding. Jesuits talk a lot about our way of proceeding, which, unlike many Ignatian values that are talked about today, is a real Ignatian term you can find in St. Ignatius' [writings]....I see this Society as one religious institute with, of course, a charismatic founder and its own way of living in community and organizing itself as a community worldwide—its own

way of doing ministry, its own way of praying, its own way of proceeding that is unique, and has many unique characteristics about it.[4]

Indeed, one of the common themes of the interviews was the "Jesuit way of proceeding," which corresponds to North's understanding of informal institutional rules. In many cases, the Jesuit way of proceeding produces visible and remarkable results. But are the formal and informal rules of the Society able to respond to disciplinary matters arising from sexual abuse and other scandalous behavior?

Many people perceive the Jesuits as an alternative to the broader Catholic Church, but the Jesuits we interviewed denied such a distinction, with one sharing:

> Often, the two organizations are seen as separate, and they're not in reality. And so, a lot of what I think about the Catholic Church is what I think about the Society because [the] Society is within the Catholic Church.... Yet we are the church. We're not the shadow church or a parish church or the other church, or I go to the Jesuits because I don't like the Catholics. It's the same thing [with] many of the same weaknesses as far as the largeness of the organization, or the shambles that leadership is often finding themselves in, or trying to translate the ideal into what it is we can actually do.[5]

While they recognized problems in the Catholic Church and the Society of Jesus, the Jesuits we interviewed recalled the words of the Formal Institute, identifying themselves as a community of friends in the Lord called together to work under the banner of the cross as soldiers for Christ and his vicar, the pope.[6]

One professor at a Jesuit university noted, "It's so easy to look at the Jesuits as the [guys in] white hats that are progressive and on the right side of every issue" before admitting that the reality is more complex.[7] A professor at a different university summed up her impression of the Jesuits in three words: strength, confidence, and accomplishment. She said, "The Jesuits know how to make things happen."[8] A teacher in one of their schools described the Jesuits as a "missionary group" seeking to empower the poor and the marginalized.[9] A professor in a Catholic university sponsored by another religious order highlighted Jesuit ministries with their outreach to the urban poor, Jesuit Relief Service, Jesuit Volunteer Corps, and the Cristo Rey Network.[10]

Nevertheless, having an excellent reputation can be a double-edged sword in organizations that are responding to sexual abuse and other scandalous behavior on the part of its members. Jesuits are keenly concerned with protecting the reputation of the Society as a whole and of its individual members. The laypeople we interviewed tended to point to the importance of the "Jesuit brand," however, the Jesuits were more likely to frame the importance of reputation in terms of mission.

When we discussed personal and institutional reputation with a group of Jesuits, the tension over reputations was apparent. Yet it was also clear that, in the end, they see reputation as critically important for the success of the Society of Jesus. One Jesuit immediately pointed to the First Principle and Foundation, which states that they should be indifferent to wealth, poverty, honor, and dishonor. He explained that he sees honor and dishonor as equivalent to having a good or bad reputation. All of their efforts should be aimed toward fulfilling the purpose of the Society, but he immediately pointed to early concerns over propriety, which he admitted reflected a sensitivity to reputation. He concluded, "We can't forget the fact that it was a reputation that led to the suppression of a Society of Jesus," referring to the politically charged period from 1773 to 1814 when Jesuit work was suspended nearly everywhere. Another Jesuit pointed out that once you have an institution, you survive on your reputation.[11]

The Jesuits referenced their founding documents and *Constitutions* as informing their perspectives throughout the interviews. Their emphasis on their origins is, at least in part, the result of following the decrees of the Second Vatican Council on religious life. The council defined the religious orders as composed of individuals and communities that have vowed to follow the evangelical counsels of chastity, poverty, and obedience. After asserting the church's authority to interpret these counsels and regulate their practice, the council declared,

> And so it has come about that, like a tree growing from a seed planted by God and spreading out its branches in a wonderful and varied way in the field of the Lord, there has grown up a variety of forms of solitary or community life and different families which increase their resources both for the progress of their members and the good of the whole Body of Christ.[12]

The First and General Examen for the Society of Jesus is in harmony with the Second Vatican Council's understanding of the purpose of a religious order. It states, "The end of the Society is to devote itself both to the salvation and perfection of its members' own souls, but also to labor strenuously in giving aid toward the salvation and perfection of the souls of their neighbors."[13] The governance structures within the Society invest the same individuals with the task of prioritizing the spiritual needs of their members as well as enforcing discipline. While such a leadership structure might be adequate for the administration of internal affairs among members, it is not adequate for responding to serious disciplinary concerns when Jesuits in their apostolic endeavors harm the people they are supposed to serve.

The Second Vatican's Decree on the Sensitive Renewal of Religious Life has also played a role in shaping how religious orders are governed and how they have responded to sexual abuse. The council defined the renewal of religious orders in terms of a constant return to the sources of Christian life in general and to the "original genius of religious foundations" (*primigeniamque institutorum*) with the "necessary modifications of such foundations to accommodate new circumstances."[14] In short, the council directed the religious orders to renew themselves by returning to founding documents such as rules, constitutions, and charters. One might also include sources such as Ignatius's *Exercises*; however, we are concentrating more on the institutional documents for obvious reasons.

Having called for modifications, the council decreed the religious orders must "reverence and embrace the genius of its founder, its authentic tradition, the whole heritage, indeed, of the religious body" (*PC* 2.b). At the same time, it stated, "All must recognize that any likely renewal derives more from a stricter adherence to the rule and the constitutions than from the creation of new legislation" (*PC* 4). Taken altogether, these statements illustrate that the decree discouraged reforms in terms of governance by framing founding documents as things to be reverenced and at the same time discouraged new legislation. Emphasizing founding documents for orders founded prior to the eighteenth century locked them into governance structures predicated on the political thought of Plato, Aristotle, and their Neoplatonic heirs.

The Society of Jesus invested a great deal of energy into implementing the Second Vatican's directives, as seen in the 1995 edition of *Constitutions of the Society of Jesus and Their Complementary Norms*. In one volume, the Jesuits published both the *Constitutions* as they were ratified in 1568 with footnotes to indicate obsolete provisions and the *Contemporary Norms*. In order to show the internal unity and ongoing spiritual identity between the *Constitutions* and the *Contemporary Norms*, the general congregation of the Society determined the two should be published side by side (*CCN* 81).

While a detailed examination of the relationship between the *Constitutions* and the *Contemporary Norms* is beyond the scope of our study, this way of presenting the laws governing the Society of Jesus poses problems, particularly when it comes to provisions in the *Constitutions* that were never abrogated. There are two examples that clearly illustrate the difficulty of reading the *Contemporary Norms* in light of the *Constitutions*. The first treats impediments to joining the Society. These impediments included apostasy, heresy, schism, homicide, infamy, and enormous sins. The *Constitutions* clarify how infamy and enormous sins should be considered:

> Infamy because of enormous sins is understood to be an impediment in the place where the sinner was declared infamous. If he should, when far from that place, give such signs of repentance that they reestablish confidence in him, he could be admitted in our Lord. Which sins of this kind are enormous and which are not will be left to the judgment of the superior general. (*CCN* 80)

The *Complementary Norms* also hold that men who have lost their reputation due to some crime committed, including homicide or participation in an abortion, or because of depraved morals, should not be admitted in the region where this occurred; however, such a man can be admitted by the superior general (*CCN* 81).

The second example is in the section on the causes for dismissal from the Society of Jesus. The *Constitutions* decree a member can be dismissed for being a scandal to others but proceeds to say that if he is good except for the scandal, "prudence will consider whether it is expedient to give him permission to go to some far-distant region of the Society, without leaving the Society" (*CCN* 98–99). Perhaps this explains the decision on the part of the Society of Jesus to move men who had sexually abused children to work with marginalized Indigenous communities in Oregon and Alaska. The rules in the *Constitutions* and the *Complementary Norms* do not cause abuse, but they foster the conditions where it can take place by concealing abuse and other seriously problematic behavior. The *Constitutions* incorporate the very best ideas of governance in the Renaissance or early modern period, but there have been significant developments in how we understand systems, structures, and institutions since the first printing of the *Constitutions* in 1559.

Describing the *Constitutions* and some of Ignatius's letters on obedience, the Jesuit historian John O'Malley provides this assessment:

> There is no getting around the fact, however, that the general teaching contained in these letters and in the *Constitutions* reflected, sometimes in exaggerated form, the prevalent sixteenth-century worldview in which the universe was ordered from the top downward, in which the benefit of every doubt was enjoyed by persons in authority, and in which both religious and secular authority was invested with a sacral character.[15]

Given this premise, the *Constitutions* emphasize the importance of discerning the qualities of anyone considered for leadership positions because they assumed bad leaders would result in bad communities and good leaders in good communities.

In the 465 years that have passed since the publication of the *Constitutions*, we have learned that the relationship between leaders and the organizations they serve is more complex than the simple top-down model. Leaders who are formed in a system are the least likely agents for positive change, and expecting them to do so—given all that we have learned about social behavior—is a form of wishful thinking. We do not deny the maxim that grace perfects nature or the idea that grace plays a role in the lives of leaders; however, relying on grace and the positive qualities of their leaders has not prevented them from making disastrous decisions that have harmed people.

The political theories that supported monarchy influenced the decision to have a superior general who is elected for life. Other leadership positions in the Society of Jesus have a fixed term, which could be a sign of a more responsive group of leaders; however, the Jesuits we spoke with indicated that the same men are cycled through different leadership positions in the Society. The early Jesuits described their governance structure as "monarchical," and it remains an apt description.

When it comes to bad superiors, a Jesuit with leadership experience said that the members have told him, "Oh, we can wait them out." Leadership terms last six years in the Society, but this participant explained that members are in the Society for the long haul.[16] Rather than challenging bad leadership, the rule is to wait it out. We heard similar sentiments from professors concerning academic deans or university presidents. Perhaps it can be explained by the type of job security that comes from tenure or a religious profession in hierarchical organizations. Still, given the central role that individual provincials and superiors play in overseeing community life, matters of discipline, apostolic works, and implementing the mission, this willingness to "wait out" bad leadership strikes us as a significant weakness. A bad leader, whether a superior or a dean, can do significant damage while members "wait out" their time. O'Malley has argued that the Jesuit monarchy was moderated in the early period in three ways. First, the general congregation, not the general, was the highest authority. Second, the *Constitutions* stipulated the limitations according to which every superior had to govern. Third, the performance of the superior general was also subject to review, and provisions were in place whereby he could be removed from office.[17] However, the superior general was vested with the authority to admit and to dismiss Jesuits, to send and to recall them from studies, to appoint and to remove rectors from colleges, and to buy or sell any movable temporal goods held by the colleges and houses of the Society.[18] Only the superior general had the authority to call a general convocation, except in those cases where there was a need to elect a new general.[19]

The *Constitutions* did provide for removing a superior general by the general congregation, but it strictly limited when he could be removed. The first reason was incapacitation through illness or advanced age. The second was for mortal sins involving external actions such as sexual sins, embezzlement, alienating property from the Society and giving it to relatives, wounding someone with a blade, and holding false doctrine. "Since those who hold an office, especially one so universal, can be calumniated by many persons for various reasons," the *Constitutions* declared, "much care must be taken that the proofs for these faults are as strong as morally possible" (*CCN* 368, 370 [777]). This presumption that the higher the officeholder, the higher the bar for allegations was, as we have seen, universal in the late medieval and early modern Catholic Church. It was also a principle that discouraged members from reporting such "mortal sins."

The founding documents stress that leaders in the Society, from the local superiors to the superior general, should prioritize the pastoral or spiritual care of the members of the Society when exercising their disciplinary function. The contemporary norms reflect this principle. After stressing the importance of the promotion of justice in the Society's mission today, Norm 15 states,

> Our institute, according to the Spirit of the *Constitutions*, with great care and without deviation in anything, but at the same time out of love and desire of all perfection, **by means of discreet charity**, under the direction of superiors, is to be applied by taking into account persons, places, and times, and other circumstances. We must always keep in mind the purpose, "which is not other than the greater divine service **and the good of those who live under this institute**." (*CCN* 66–67; emphasis ours)

Superiors, who have both pastoral and administrative roles, are directed to make decisions concerning members out of love and by discreet charity.

Obviously, superiors and provincials do not always act out of love, but there is an expectation that they should respond to disciplinary matters with love and mercy. *The Constitutions and Complementary Norms* provide conditions for dismissal, which is reserved to provincials and the superior general. Provincials can dismiss novices and those who have professed simple vows, but only the superior general can dismiss Jesuits who have professed solemn vows.[20] Even when a member has acted egregiously enough to be dismissed, the *Constitutions* direct those who have the authority to dismiss to act with "discreet zeal."[21]

The rule is that the provincials and superior general should only dismiss members when it is necessary.[22] The *Constitutions* direct the men who have the power to dismiss members to rid themselves of all affection before making such a decision and to base their decisions on the greater divine glory, the common good, and the good of the individual as far as is possible.[23] These criteria are vague and allow for a great deal of discretion on the part of the decision-makers. The reluctance to dismiss the fully professed Jesuit is understandable when you consider it generally takes at least eight years before a man is fully professed into the Society, but the *Constitutions* fail to recognize how difficult it is for people to put aside all of their feelings for someone who was a mentor, protégé, or close companion for years.

Normally, disciplinary matters are reported to a superior before being reported to the provincial, and in the case of the professed Jesuits, to the superior general—all of whom are expected to practice discretion, whether charitable or zealous. At each level, information flows to a single individual who decides whether to share the information with consultors or forward it up the chain of command. The *Constitutions* state that "the consent or advice of consultors is never required to act validly, apart from those cases specified in the law."[24]

Jesuits holding leadership positions have a great deal of latitude as to when they should call upon consultors. The primary exception related to our study is that the superior general must include his consultors in decisions to dismiss Jesuits who have professed their vows.[25] When consultors are included in deliberations over discipline, they are bound by confidentiality. The norms advise superiors to "show justified severity" toward consultors who inappropriately communicate to others what took place in a consultation.[26]

As we have seen, laws, policies, norms, and other legal documents only have the status of rules (institutions) when they are truly normative in an organization. The structures established by *The Constitutions and Complementary Norms* leave enormous leeway in decision-making to a few members of the Society in matters of discipline. They also establish clear rules, framed in pastoral categories, to maintain secrecy and confidentiality in all disciplinary matters. These are all conditions that make sexual abuse more likely, but we wanted to establish the degree to which these provisions in *The Constitutions and Complementary Norms* actually guide disciplinary decisions. We were also looking for the conditions that create disincentives to report problems, such as power differentials, lack of transparency, and patronage.

FRATERNAL CORRECTION

In the first part of this book, we showed that informal rules frequently have greater weight in an organization and are quite effective at resisting and undermining new laws, charters, or policies. The Jesuit way of proceeding has many informal rules that are grounded in the idea of Christian fraternity, which has helped the Society to foster a real sense of mutual support and community; nonetheless, we found evidence that the informal rules around patronage and fraternal correction can create the conditions where discipline breaks down.

As the interviews progressed, we found evidence of disincentives to report, but more importantly, we learned how informal rules related to "fraternal correction" amplify power differentials, mute transparency, and reinforce patronage. The Royal Commission did not discuss fraternal correction but did recommend that "the Holy See should amend canon law to ensure that the 'pastoral approach' is not an essential precondition to the commencement of canonical action relating to child sexual abuse."[27] In response, the Australian Catholic Bishops Conference stated, "There is no obligation in canon law to attempt a 'pastoral approach' before commencing a canonical action relating to sexual abuse of a child or young person."[28] It is clear that neither the Royal Commission nor the Australian bishops recognized the existence or role of informal rules associated with the idea of fraternal correction in disciplinary matters.

The rules associated with fraternal correction are grounded in the New Testament and have created an obstacle for reformers since at least the sixth century.[29] The source is Matthew 18:15–20, where Jesus says to the disciples,

> If another member of the church sins against you, go and point out the fault when the two of you are alone. If the member listens to you, you have regained that one. But if you are not listened to, take one or two others along with you, so that every word may be confirmed by the evidence of two or three witnesses. If the member refuses to listen to them, tell it to the church, let such a one be to you as a Gentile and a tax collector. Truly I tell you whatever you bind on earth will be bound in heaven, and whatever you loose on earth will be loosed in heaven. Again, truly I tell you, if two of you agree on earth about anything you ask, it will be done for you by my Father in Heaven. For wherever two or three are gathered in my name, I am there among them.

This passage has been interpreted as a general rule for Christians, but this is a case where context matters.

Matthew 18 is an extended discussion of the duties and responsibilities of those who would be leaders in the church as opposed to the little ones (Matt 18:1–14). Addressing the disciples, Jesus opens the discussion of leadership with this warning:

> If any of you put a stumbling block before one of these little ones who believe in me, it would be better for you if a great

> millstone were fastened around your neck and you were drowned in the depth of the sea. Woe to the world because of stumbling blocks! Occasions for stumbling are bound to come, but woe to the one by whom the stumbling block comes! (Matt 18:6–7)

"Stumbling block" could also be translated as "scandal." So, this discussion of leadership opens with a warning that scandalous leaders face divine judgment for their actions. Jesus told the disciples that the angels would report how they treated the little ones (Matt 18:10). "So, it is not the will of your Father in heaven," Christ reminded the disciples, "that one of these little ones should be lost" (Matt 18:14).

Jesus was neither teaching that victims must privately confront people in power who have harmed them nor requiring them to find multiple witnesses before making a charge. Instead, Christ instructed those who have power how they should respond to people who have sinned against them—as leaders—in the church. The passage does not provide guidance as to how Christian leaders should respond when members of the church sin against vulnerable and marginalized members of the community. Christ was not so much presenting a model of fraternal correction as a model of pastoral correction for sins against the pastor.

This idea of fraternal correction has been used to silence people, but the Doctor of Reform, Peter Damian, rejected this reading in the eleventh century. He pointed to the example of St. Paul, who publicly rebuked St. Peter at the Jerusalem Council in Acts 15:10–11 as an example of a precedent for publicizing the crimes of the clergy.[30] Indeed, he also pointed to Numbers 25:4, when the Lord commanded Moses to take all of the leaders and hang them publicly, as evidence that highly placed people in the church must be vigorously prosecuted and publicly punished for their crimes to demonstrate the church's commitment to justice. If the clergy failed to exercise proper discipline, he argued the laity had the right to take away both their power and their money.[31]

To be clear, we are not arguing for withholding forgiveness. Forgiveness—not policing a community for predators—is the central theme of Matthew 18. When Peter asks how many times he should forgive those who sin against him, Jesus responds seventy-seven times (Matt 18:22). Should sexual predators be forgiven seventy-seven times? That is the wrong question. Frankly, if a perpetrator commits such an act multiple times, the community that enabled the repetition of the offenses is complicit in those crimes. Yet repeat offenses too often happen because the same person is responsible for both pastoral care and discipline. Not every "sin" should be handled in the same way.

Pastoral care emphasizes being patient and merciful, which in some circumstances is certainly appropriate. However, in disciplinary matters, the emphasis on pastoral care enables problems ranging from inferior performance to sexual assault. As a member of a different religious order told us, there is a confusion between what is simply sinful and what is criminal. People can be and should be forgiven their sins even if they must be removed from their positions or incarcerated for their crimes.

It is one thing for a religious order to choose fraternal correction as the disciplinary approach to handle internal issues that arise between members of its community. It is quite another to fall back on fraternal correction when the victims of the misbehavior are individuals outside of the community—particularly in cases involving children and vulnerable adults. In such cases, those on the receiving end of misdeeds did not agree to live by the code of the community. Fraternal correction, with its emphasis on pastoral care, may work for addressing divisions resulting from sins involving gossip, insults, or lies; however, it is not the proper response to criminal acts such as slander, sexual assault, or murder. Religious orders and the church at large must utilize a stricter approach to protect those outside of their communities from the predators within them.

Church leaders fall far short even by the standards set in Matthew 18. When fraternal correction fails and ordained offenders refuse to listen, leaders have not always shared the offense with the broader community, as we have increasingly learned since the *Boston Globe* reports starting in 2002, dramatized in the film *Spotlight*. The church does not practice the transparency called for by Jesus Christ. Instead, as our participants confirmed, church leaders protect offenders from embarrassment by keeping disciplinary matters secret. With respect to privacy, fraternal correction is effective. Fraternal correction and the inclination to avoid embarrassment manifests an underlying emphasis on pastoral care.

The priority pastoral care places on privacy and secrecy clearly emerges out of an institutional commitment to reputation. Unfortunately, in too many instances, the priority placed on pastoral care results in a preferential option for the perpetrator. This is true whether the offender is a lay, religious, or ordained employee; however, religious orders prioritize their members in the same way that bishops prioritize their priests. In short, there is less concern with protecting the privacy of employees who are not ordained. The consequence is that both the ordained and the religious are held to lower standards in terms of morality and performance, even though they hold leadership positions.

Institutional analysis makes it clear that pastoral care and discipline must be carried out separately. In some matters, with some sins, a pastoral approach toward the perpetrator is not only wrong, but destructive. While it is true that prioritizing a pastoral response to disciplinary matters involving sexual abuse is not a provision of canon law, it is central to the Jesuit way of proceeding and is deeply embedded in Catholic culture. The rules associated with fraternal correction lead to perverse outcomes. An example of a perverse outcome is, as one Jesuit shared with us, that the more offensive the behavior, the more likely it is to be kept secret. We were dismayed to hear a Jesuit who has served in leadership put it this way: "The brother has a right to be protected." Another Jesuit said a Jesuit was entitled "to have his privacy protected, and it's a real responsibility [for superiors] to do that."

A commitment to fraternal correction is inculcated in the formation process, and its effects undermine the Jesuits' ability to screen their members properly. This was something we did not expect to find. Like all of the non-Jesuit participants we interviewed, we had what was, in retrospect, an idealized view of the Society of Jesus's formation program. While their formation is longer and more involved than that of the diocesan clergy, the formal and informal rules create significant holes for screening out inappropriate candidates.

The discussion of formation came up after a former provincial shared that the Jesuits rely heavily on fraternal correction to respond to disciplinary issues. He continued, "When someone says, 'You know you have to do something because Father so and so did this.' The better superiors—your first response is, 'Well, have you talked it over with him?'" Another Jesuit in the group immediately responded,

> What [the former provincial] just mentioned, which is ideal, seems not to have happened. Or superiors have not been willing to take on those conversations, and it doesn't seem clear to me that the imagination of what havoc these guys wreak on the people of God is taken very much into consideration. And I'm thinking about who gets ordained and who

> is sent out on the people of God, and you just think, "Well, wait, what was going on here…." It's a pretty broad gate that we continue to use….So that's been very disheartening to me, sometimes in the Society people are trusting wrongly that time will take care of it or just enough prayer will make this person serviceable or usable in the field, and you just think, "Wow, I don't think that [fraternal correction] happened."[32]

This distinction between what ideally should happen and what in reality does happen was a recurring theme.

Responding to the statement that fraternal correction does not happen led another member of the group to explain the difficulty of practicing fraternal correction as a Jesuit who has less standing than the Jesuits around him:

> So yes, we do fraternal correction. I've been through a number of communities where we correct, we admonish, we try to bring awareness of a situation to a concerned member, but all I found in my experience that the reaction is, "Who are you to say that to me?" and, "Go to the superior if you need to."…So, whether it's because I am a Jesuit of color, a JOC, or because I'm younger in the formation system, or because I'm culturally from a different place, then we don't have equal authority among the brothers [in] the fraternal community.[33]

The lack of equality presents significant disincentives for Jesuits who have less standing due to their race, cultural background, or age to report disciplinary problems.

This Jesuit of color gave an example of fraternal correction breaking down in the case of a Jesuit who was a reckless driver. He asked how many car crashes it takes for a superior to pull a member's driver's license. He told us of a member who had multiple car crashes but was not disciplined until he had an accident that left another Jesuit so seriously injured that he had to be intubated. He presented fraternal correction as an aspect of his call, saying, "Again, the sense of whistleblowing and being called to task for whistleblowing that's very real. We live it, so we do take the risks and that's part I think of really just life and community and fraternal love that we take the hits when we do call people to account."[34] The question is whether everyone is as committed to taking the risk. More fundamentally, how could we assess whether people share the commitment to whistleblowing?

Another member of the group drew out the tensions between fraternal correction and fraternity. He indicated that many members are reluctant to engage in this type of confrontation:

> This problem that we have, I think it's the other side of the sense of fraternity—the strong sense of fraternity that we have and support of each other...for strong as most of Jesuits are, we're also quite conflict averse in many ways. People will avoid a conflict by either not seeing it, by turning away, by sort of thinking that it's the superior's problem...but again I don't know that that's peculiar. I think most people are conflict averse and engaging in those kinds of honest conversations can sometimes be really difficult.[35]

He said the Jesuits have this rule from their spiritual formation to try to put the best interpretation on people's words and actions, which is a good thing in terms of spiritual direction, but it can also be used to avoid conflict.

An example from the beginnings of the Society can help illustrate the point. Before the Jesuits were formally established, Peter Faber became a priest thanks to Ignatius's encouragement. His ministry has unquestionably shaped the development Jesuits over the centuries, leading in part to his canonization by Pope Francis in 2013. In a letter to a young man planning on entering the Society, Faber elaborated on the concept of fraternal charity. Much of the letter describes how members of the Society should put the Order before themselves, preserving peace and unity among the members. Yet, we would argue, the spiritual discipline he enumerates could perpetuate a culture of conflict aversion.

Many of his points can be understood through the spiritual lens of self-denial and self-reflection. Faber writes, for example, that members "should always will, defend, make the best case for, and advocate what your brother wills—struggling always against your own opinion and judgement and doing your brother's will instead."[36] When disagreements arise, Faber writes, members should not oppose each other.

> Even though you might consider your reasons for opposing him imminently just, tell yourself in reply that you have no just cause for so confidently assenting to your own judge-

ment and so readily rejecting the other's view as wrong. Go on to reflect on how unjust of you it is to allow any animosity or indignation to arise within you for no prior reason and to turn aside from the peace, goodwill and loving inclination you once so well conceived toward your brother—a thing you should certainly value more highly than your own judgement and self-will, especially to the degree that no matter of faith or morals is necessary for salvation is at stake.[37]

An overarching theme of the letter, in the interest of maintaining "brotherly concord," is to refrain from judging other members but instead for brothers to examine themselves. But it verges on the extreme when, for example, Faber writes, "Never pay attention to your brothers' faults (unless you happen to be responsible for their direction and correction)."[38] Fraternal charity understood in this way provides multiple justifications for avoiding conflict and minimizing bad behavior.

The Jesuits we interviewed identified the difficulty of practicing fraternal correction as a human problem rather than a Jesuit problem. We agree. Most people, for better or for worse, are not formed in a culture that teaches people should always think the best of other people. On the contrary, most people are raised to be discerning if not outright suspicious when it comes to the claims of others. This is obvious from the proverbs we use. "The proof is in the pudding." "Don't believe everything you hear; only believe half of what you see and nothing at all until it's proven to be true." "All that glitters is not gold." "Let the buyer beware." "A fool and his money are soon parted." Certainly, fraternal correction is a difficult practice for human beings to follow, but it is more difficult in a community that promotes thinking the best of each other as a rule.

Expecting fraternal correction to work as a form of governance, which is a broader Catholic commitment, is a manifestation of what the sociologist Mark Chaves calls the religious congruence fallacy. The fallacy is the expectation of consistency among an individual's beliefs and attitudes as well as between their religious beliefs and behavior across contexts and situations.[39] Chaves showed that decades of research in anthropology, sociology, and psychology demonstrate that such congruence is rare and only exists in very specific contexts.

More specifically, the fallacy is that religious congruence is common. Chaves was careful to distinguish the fallacy from hypocrisy or religious insincerity because it refers to our expectations of others rather than their behavior.[40] While it is beyond the scope of this book, we believe we could make a strong case that the Society of Jesus has a great deal of religious congruence in many matters; however, they have not all internalized their beliefs to the same extent and neither they nor we should operate with the expectation that they have. In other words, not everyone practices what they preach. Indeed, this is why organizations need rules, structures, and systems to surface problems and to ensure they are being addressed.

In our study, we learned that simply voicing a concern does not ensure it will be handled properly. The Jesuits we interviewed, for example, revealed they did not expect to learn the outcome when a disciplinary matter is reported to a superior or provincial. When we asked how they would respond if they reported something without any apparent result, there was a range of opinions. One Jesuit said that he would assume the superior had done the right thing and had more information about the situation than he had, though he added he would take the matter to the provincial if he were deeply concerned. Another described the lack of feedback in these types of situations as undermining many members' trust in the system.[41]

A retired Jesuit recalled that he had reported a member who suffered due to rheumatoid arthritis and had developed an addiction to Oxycontin. He said the man had to use several radio alarms at full volume to wake up, and when he left for a trip, he forgot to turn them off. When our participant and another Jesuit went into the room, they found "this whole pharmacopeia—just bottle after bottle of Oxycontin." He continued,

> So, the two of us talked to three levels of superiors: provincial, rector, and the guy in charge of parishes. And they all said, "Yeah, we know there's a problem we'll talk to him." All they would do was talk to him, and he would say, "Well, I'll try to do better...." And eventually, he died in an accident that I'm sure was caused by his being on Oxycontin. He had a bad fall, hit his head on a radiator, was unconscious for a month, and died at a young age. You know, sometimes you do reveal something to superiors, and nothing is done.[42]

He went on to state that sometimes the superiors act and intervene when a Jesuit is in trouble, but the overall sense was that there is very little information shared with those who report disciplinary matters.

A former rector and superior shared that it was rare but not unheard of for him to receive a complaint or concern regarding a member's behavior from within the community. He said information about misbehavior tended to come from outside when the member was traveling or giving a retreat somewhere.[43] Others reported that they found out about problems from the housekeeping staff or from administrators in schools, universities, and other organizations sponsored by the Society of Jesus. This was a repeating theme. "Because people in the Jesuits have a strong sense of mission, they can easily become focused on the mission and not enough on companionship," a former superior said, "and there's a strong initiative underway by our leadership coming all the way from the general in Rome to try to overcome that problem. And it's not a disastrously bad problem, but it's a problem."[44]

For an organization that relies heavily on pastoral care concepts like fraternal correction and charitable discretion in its internal discipline, such breakdowns in companionship may indeed be disastrous. If the Jesuits are unaware and uninvolved in the lives of the men in their community, they have no real oversight or functional accountability structures. At the same time, in communities in which the rector or superior tends to micromanage, members suffer a different form of dysfunction that can also create disincentives to report. If good superiors promote healthy communities, which our Jesuit participants generally affirmed, we asked how the Society handles problematic rectors, superiors, or provincials.

As you might imagine, the more rank-and-file Jesuits had little knowledge as to how problematic leaders are handled. But two of our participants had some experience with disciplining people in leadership and removing them from their positions. Their responses are worth quoting at length. The first reported:

> I've seen a couple of situations where local superiors have been removed before their office came to an end. There's normally a six-year term if you're going to be a local superior. It's been because of the community talking to the provincial and saying this is not working and the provincial, I think, then intervenes in some way, probably talking with the general. But it's not an easy process to remove somebody, and I don't think there's any formal procedure for it. But it's through the process of manifestation of what's going on and talking to the leadership. And leaders can take action if they want

> to, or if they decide that it's necessary. I've seen it happen a few times, with local superiors in Jesuit communities being removed before their term was over, and it's painful, but it happens, and it has to be a pretty bad situation for it to get that far but it's not unknown.[45]

The first thing we noticed is the Jesuit did not really know how the process worked when a superior had to be removed. He mentioned the manifestation, which is when the provincial visits and talks to the members of their communities, but the process appears to be opaque. Moreover, the informal rule is that provincials do not get involved until a situation has gotten to be "pretty bad." Insofar as it is a process at all, it is completely dependent on the judgment of the provincial and perhaps the general.

The second Jesuit, who had experience with how the Society responds to bad leaders, made an important distinction between the process for disciplining superiors or provincials as opposed to Jesuits who are presidents of universities. He discussed a president of a Jesuit university who has a mistress but who was an excellent fundraiser and explained that it is "very, very, very, difficult as rector if you have a rotten president who is a Jesuit." When pressed about how the Society responded to problematic leaders, he continued,

> It depends on how problematic. There have been people who've been removed from presidencies. There have been people who have been removed from being provincial. There have been rectors who would normally serve a six-year term who instead have served three or four. And there are times the order says we just can't do this anymore. But usually, they will try to see if there's a way you can be helpful with some people. But the folks who are going to be problematic are already beginning with that isolation I talked to you about. And so, what you try to do is to get someone on the ground where they may help this person become less isolated. That's how I think they tried to do it generally. Or they'll send someone to say you know, can we send somebody who can be helpful here?[46]

Clearly, the Society does exercise oversight and disciplines leaders, which is important to recognize; however, their first response seems to be a pastoral response of providing more support and an opportunity to change their behavior, except in cases that might involve scandal.

PATRONAGE

Patronage plays a role in who gets disciplined and how. When we asked whether patronage impacts promotions and discipline, it became clear that one must distinguish between the apostolic works performed by the Jesuits, such as serving as a president in a Jesuit university or editor of a Jesuit journal, and the internal leadership structures. One participant pointed to a particular Jesuit university president as an example of someone who has groomed Jesuits to take on leadership roles in Jesuit higher education, but the sense is that Jesuits in higher education develop their own bases of power with donors to colleges and universities.[47] The same can be true of high school presidents.

The discussion of patronage within the Society's leadership structures followed a pattern we saw with the discussion of fraternal correction. At the outset, the Jesuits we interviewed reported that patronage used to be a real concern in the Society, but that it had substantially diminished. A senior Jesuit reported,

> I feel like the patronage piece, it's changing, or it's changed over my life in the Society, I think because over thirty years ago there was still a kind of golden person phenomenon. There were some people who, because of something, the power of their charisma, the connection they had with somebody, they seemed to be special, so they stood outside the ordinary course of things, you know, in terms of how people did a certain kind of period of study.[48]

He said he found this type of patronage to have been very destructive because it meant that "some people are more equal than others." While such patronage may be diminished in the provinces in the United States, an African Jesuit reported that patronage remains a serious issue there.[49] We think it is important to recall that several Jesuits pointed out that members are not equal due to their seniority, age, race, and national origin, even if patronage is less of a problem than in the past.

One of the Jesuits responded by saying he felt that patronage had shifted away from the personal connections to an ideological form.

"Sometimes, it is like a shadow formation for people that become really alienated about what the Society is as opposed to what they think it should be."[50] "Shadow formation" is a term that is quite familiar to the faculties of seminaries and theological schools. It refers to priests and religious outside of the seminary system who encourage seminarians to ignore the instruction they are receiving mostly of moral or liturgical matters, but there are any number of issues that such shadow formation can center around, such as opposition to a pope and his policies.

This statement led to an interesting discussion of Jesuit formation. An international Jesuit reported that there is still a type of "Golden Jesuit" patronage that takes place in formation when some Jesuits get the prime assignments in their "experiments," which provide novitiates opportunities to exercise different forms of ministry. He said, "The Society's formation program is long enough, at least ten years, even up to twelve or thirteen years, that my own experience of the golden persons in formation, I've seen them drop off the grid as the formation process proceeds. There will be the few survivors, and they do very well." Even though he admitted that a few people do benefit from personal patronage, he explained that he was confident that the length of the formation process takes care of the problem through natural attrition.[51]

There was a tendency that came up in all of our interviews with Jesuits to recognize the existence of benign patronage in the form of mentorship. Some pointed to academic mentors who help Jesuit scholastics become scholars in different fields. "There [are] occasional situations where somebody in a position of authority has somebody who they were nurturing along or mentoring and so forth, but it's not exactly the patronage system," this former rector reported before concluding, "I would say it is not the dominant system in the Society of Jesus."[52] He described the overall formation process as collaborative and interactive, but he admitted there are exceptional cases of "Golden Jesuits" where patronage plays a role in advancement. In a different interview, a Jesuit said that there is patronage in the Society but described it in terms of superiors identifying gifts of nature and graces and then fitting men into the best possible ministry.[53] Another said that in religious circles, patronage could become an issue whenever a person proves to be a really effective mentor.[54]

Patronage is not necessarily a bad thing, as our participants pointed out in the case of mentorship. However, it does create conflicts of interest when it comes to administrative matters involving discipline. As we saw earlier in the Cardinal McCarrick report, a patronage relationship makes it easier to minimize and explain away bad behavior. When we asked if there was an expectation of recusal for a superior who has had a relationship with a member, either as a mentor or as a mentee, when a disciplinary decision involving that member arose, none of the Jesuits we interviewed said there was such an expectation.

In addition to the types of entanglements that emerge from patronage, there is the closeness of the men who belong to the order. Several Jesuits referred to belonging to the Society as belonging to a family. Others were a bit more reserved:

> Well, I wouldn't use the term *family*. I use the term *companions*....I mean, that's what *society* means [*compañia*] companions, so it's not the same kind of relationship that I would have with members of my family. Because it has all sorts of other dimensions to it connected with work and connected with mission and all of that sort of stuff.[55]

Another described the Society of Jesus as a mission in companionship and as a community of friends in the Lord, which was affirmed by one of the other Jesuits in that interview.[56] Whether they see themselves as family or as companions, their relationships complicate their work in schools and universities, which have policies that are not always consistent with the Jesuit way of proceeding.

We asked how they handled situations in an academic setting where they had an administrative role over other Jesuits in organizations with policies and rules that did not align with Jesuit rules. It became clear that these were very difficult situations for them. One reported,

> We're not going to deal with each other in a legalistic way because we don't have that kind of a rule in place...if it were another Jesuit reporting to me, I would have to straddle the two, as a brother, and at the same time, as one bound to the institution, so it's not as easy or clear cut. Two sets of rules get complicated when a Jesuit is an administrator over another Jesuit in a university. It's not clear-cut.[57]

This led another to respond,

> I would take a little different tack, speaking as a former dean, and say we don't have two faculty handbooks. There was one

> faculty handbook, and my staff was really amazed because previous deans who weren't Jesuits would tend to give a pass because they were afraid of taking action against a Jesuit.[58]

While we do not doubt this Jesuit treated both Jesuit and non-Jesuit faculty the same way, the fact that his staff was amazed shows how rare it is for Jesuit faculty to be held to the same standards as everyone else. The informal rule is that they should be treated in a deferential manner as possible.

Beyond these binary responses, other Jesuits affirmed the difficulty of supervising each other in academic organizations. One equated it to a familial relationship in which a dean had to supervise a spouse. Of course, most universities have policies against spouses supervising each other or have procedures for recusal when there are conflicts of interest. In general, organizations recognize nepotism as problematic.

The impetus to treat each other in a pastoral manner means they have to "straddle" Jesuit rules and the rules of the organizations they sponsor. It seems that the pastoral dimension of their relationships and governance structures ultimately drives their disciplinary processes and decisions, including protecting the privacy of those who violate rules in schools and universities.

The pastoral imperative leads some Jesuits to involve themselves in issues related to their members that appear like special treatment or consideration. Faculty and administrators at the Jesuit schools and universities reported efforts to influence decisions from matters related to the academic performance of Jesuit students in graduate programs to boundary violations of Jesuits teaching in high schools. As to the former, a department chair in a Jesuit university told us,

> There's a Jesuit safety net, isn't there? I think that we just need to put that out there....When we had a Jesuit we were having problems with, there was a lot of interest coming from the Jesuit residents, and from the president's office, and from others about why are you having a problem with this person....We did have one person [a Jesuit] who wasn't making progress on his dissertation, God bless him....We bent over backwards for him in ways that we just don't for others, so again, I think there's a level of security and deference given to folks because of the connection to the Society that wouldn't exist for others.[59]

In this case, the president was Jesuit. A program director at another Jesuit university said there used to be more differential treatment of Jesuits and laypeople but that there has been a great effort "to at least move towards equity." However, he said there is still differential treatment due to what he termed the "owner-operator problem" in Jesuit universities.[60]

The tendency for differential treatment is also an issue in Jesuit schools, which is particularly problematic given they are working with minors. One lay administrator shared a story about a Jesuit whom she described as the "king of normative power" at her high school:

> He was not abusing anyone. I want to be very clear about that, but he was crossing boundaries because he thought it was 1970, and you can play favorites and [give them] candy, touch them on the shoulder, and that kind of thing....It's not appropriate, and it went on too long because there's not a lot of Jesuits around anymore, and we knew so many people loved him. And then, when we eventually had to let him go, that had to be in consultation with the provincial...if the boundary-breaking is consistent and doesn't stop, as it was in this case, then we have to remove the person, clergy or not. But it took too long because this person is a clergy member.[61]

An interview with a principal of a Jesuit high school also affirmed that there was differential treatment of Jesuits when it came to issues such as boundary issues with students and with staff:

> So, let's say, for example, in terms of sexual abuse a lay teacher is found to have done—that teacher is excised from the community. [If] it's a Jesuit, that's family. That Jesuit is protected. That Jesuit has a life. It may not be a pleasant life, but he would just [be] taken care of by the other Jesuits when the layperson is cut loose. So, they are treated differently. In terms of other matters, they are treated differently. They can say things and do things that are taken care of on another level.[62]

Though he noted that the local superior or province could sanction Jesuit administrators and faculty members, given the Jesuit way of proceeding, he would never know whether there were sanctions or what they were.

What was clear from the interviews is that the conditions that foster sexual abuse and its concealment are present within the Society of Jesus and in their schools and universities. Their monarchical form of government is one aspect of the problem. Governance relies on the virtues of people in leadership, but even the Jesuits recognize that there is a wide range of people who hold leadership positions. Jesuits in leadership appoint their own consultors, who may be friends, mentors, or ideological allies. There are no transparent processes for evaluating men in leadership.

We did learn that there is a process of soliciting the opinions and assessments of rank-and-file members of their superiors and of men being considered for leadership positions, but the minister general or provincial decides who gets asked those opinions; moreover, people who receive these requests must keep it secret that they were asked for their assessment. The results of the process are also confidential.

CONCLUSION

We began this project with a strong sense of admiration for the Society of Jesus, and our admiration for the Jesuits remains strong. Nonetheless, the Jesuits need to find ways to address their tendency to fall into the trap of wishful thinking when it comes to governance and administration. We heard that if a man in leadership is healthy and if communities are healthy, the governance structures and the rules or the Jesuit way of proceeding are effective in promoting the salvation of its members and providing material and spiritual aid to their neighbors; we also heard that there is a whole range of people in leadership and that communities are not always healthy.

The idea that a state would be better if only it had better leaders is part of the dynamic of the capability trap. It distorts structural weak points and prevents fragile states from making sustainable progress. When it comes to the church, this evergreen optimism for "better leaders" is part of the clericalism trap. Such wishful thinking prevents Catholic organizations, including the Jesuits, from implementing sustainable reforms to address sexual abuse. Sustainable reform requires institutional reform, which is defined as the reform of formal and informal rules. To be sure, there is a need for structural reforms; however, if structural reform neglects to address the underlying rules of the game, it may only result in creating mimics.

Because rules and structures are entangled realities with complex interactions, our suggestions as to structural changes in governance will be limited. Our focus is on the formal and informal institutions (rules), some of which are contained in the *Constitutions* and the *Norms*, that need to be modified, abandoned, or replaced. Religious orders must find rules and structural expressions for their ideals and spiritual aspirations. Yet, as we learned in our interviews, there is a tendency among some Jesuits to conflate the *Exercises* with the *Constitutions* without distinguishing between Ignatius's ideals and his historical context. Altering "the Jesuit way" of proceeding will be challenging for some members of the Society.[63]

The rules related to secrecy or confidentiality also need to be abandoned when it comes to Jesuits who harm people. Certainly, there is a place for charitable discretion and there are forums that call for confidentiality, but there must be limits to charitable discretion and the Jesuits should create transparent forums to address harmful behavior and actions. The Society of Jesus must establish an alternative juridical or disciplinary structure that is not guided solely by pastoral principles toward the perpetrator, which would entail significant independence from the superiors and provincials. Success would require implementing new rules as to when Jesuits should recuse themselves from overseeing disciplinary matters involving people who have been patrons, mentors, friends, or protégés.

Given the influence of patronage, the Society ought to allow all members to vote for those who would have this juridical or administrative role. The people in this structure would also have the task of providing the results of an investigation to those who reported problems and, in cases where it is appropriate, would provide information to the public. Because the existing rules are deeply embedded, the Society would be wise to establish third-party accountability structures composed of laypeople as well as some Jesuits to assess whether new rules and structures are being effectively implemented.

In short, the Jesuits need to reevaluate their governance system in light of contemporary ideas, cultural patterns, and the prevailing social climate as Vatican II dictated. They should recognize the inherent difficulty of adapting to contemporary culture while simultaneously attempting to promote "a stricter adherence to the rule and the constitutions than from the creation of new legislation." Rules and constitutions that emerged in a sixteenth-century cultural context are ill-suited to function in a twenty-first–century context where people question authorities, investigate their decisions, and publicize scandals using traditional and social media platforms.

Their monarchical form of government creates bottlenecks for information at each level of governance. Robert Hurley, an expert on organizational trust, has identified how secrecy creates an institutional learning disability. This learning disability is preventing the members of the Society from (1) perceiving the extent of gaps between desired and actual behaviors, (2) analyzing those gaps and inventing solutions to address them, and (3) implementing those solutions through processes, procedures, routines, rules, and structural changes.[64] Hurley argued that such secrecy leads to a loss of dynamic capacity, or an organization's "capacity to reconfigure itself to adjust to changes in the environment."[65] We believe there is enough talent and commitment among the members to do just that. If they had more access to information concerning sexual abuse and made use of the insights of both the people who support their mission and those who benefit from their apostolic efforts, they could discern effective solutions.

We suggest the Society of Jesus revise its norms in light of the rule to love their neighbors as themselves. This rule denies the legitimacy of prioritizing the good of those "who live under this institute" over the needs of their neighbors. Pope John Paul II wrote that Catholics should ask themselves, "To whom should I become a neighbor?" The pope's answer was that the Christian must "become the neighbor to anyone who is in need."[66] If this is true, the Society of Jesus must rigorously assess how well their formal and informal rules protect marginalized and vulnerable people, whether they are within the Society or not, as well as their enforcement mechanisms. Since the Jesuit rules reflect those of the wider Catholic Church, the other religious orders would be wise to also engage in an assessment of their formal and informal rules.

CHAPTER 6

HOW CLERICALISM LIMITS CAPACITY

The Catholic Church treats ordained and lay employees differently. One example of note is the annual report from Georgetown's Center for Applied Research in the Apostolate (known as CARA) on the priests being ordained in the United States.[1] The report is conducted on behalf of the U.S. Conference of Catholic Bishops' Secretariat of Clergy, Consecrated Life, and Vocations. It includes details like ordinands' age, race, ethnicity, country of birth, family background, and experience in Catholic and religious education. In 2024, 392 of the 475 men ordained to the priesthood participated in the study. There is no annual study conducted about lay Catholics in the United States that parallels this yearly survey of new priests despite the fact that—from parishes to chanceries to seminaries—lay Catholics who work for the church far outnumber the ordained, including those serving our children and young people.

Clearly, it would be senseless to contemplate the church's capacity to carry out its mission without considering the critical roles played by both lay and ordained employees. As we analyzed the interviews, we added the term *capacity* as a code because we found references to rules and practices that undercut effectiveness in Catholic organizations. In this context, *capacity* refers to the ability of the church to serve the poor, advocate for the oppressed, educate, and evangelize. What affects the capacity of specifically lay employees to be effective has more impact on operations than people realize.

We were primarily concentrating on the ways that clericalism, understood as the idealization of the priesthood, created the conditions for scandal that have led so many members to exit the church; however, we also discovered that clericalism significantly impacts the church in terms of personnel in two ways.[2] First, it corrupts the process of selecting, forming, and approving candidates for the priesthood. Second, it generates tremendous churn for lay employees through what several participants called toxic workplaces in dioceses and church-sponsored organizations.

Since the people who reported this churn were engaged in one way or another with working with children, youth, and young adults, we believe it deserves some attention. We see the ongoing loss of capacity in these areas as alarming and infuriating. The Catholic Church cannot function without its lay employees, most of whom are also baptized and confirmed Catholics. We cannot learn about the effects of clericalism on capacity without hearing their voices, which is why we are sharing their experiences before sharing what we heard about seminary formation.

HOW CLERICALISM IMPACTS CAPACITY FOR LAY EMPLOYEES

We found many parallels between the experiences of lay employees working for Catholic organizations more broadly with those working for the Jesuits. There is a culture of conflict avoidance that undermines the training and development of personnel as well as the rigorous vetting of initiatives. Patronage plays a role in who gets hired and promoted. It also plays a role in who gets disciplined or fired. The difference is that laypeople who work for the church do not have the type of mutual support and aid that our Jesuit participants found in the Society of Jesus. The Jesuits we spoke with acknowledged that there are times when a community might develop some toxic characteristics, but overall, they reported having mostly good experiences in a variety of settings. The laypeople we interviewed, who worked in diocesan settings and in national organizations and are not members of religious orders, reported a workplace that often burns through employees in as little as two to three years. We note, too, that when a layperson is fired, potentially an entire family has lost income and health benefits. When a clergy member loses a position, he still gets room, board, and medical coverage.

We are not management experts, but we can confidently assert that the most important resource an organization has is its personnel. The people we interviewed generally agreed that the church does not hire the best people—clergy or lay—in our organizations. It is not that the church hires unqualified employees, but that it hires young people for positions that require more experience. This might work if it invested in their professional development, but the participants who work with national organizations said they rarely see such investments in employees.[3]

One who worked with a national organization identified clericalism as the reason the church does not invest more in lay employees. "We'll say we want to follow business [practices]," he reported, "but we're not going to actually follow the business procedures of putting the best people in place because we have so many other rules about who can have what role and that's where the clericalism comes back in."[4] Leadership roles are reserved for priests whether they have the requisite experience or education to succeed. This also means that there are limited career opportunities for advancement when working for Catholic organizations.

Another participant claimed Catholic hiring practices are biased toward less qualified people. Pointing to the way parishes hire as an example, she said, "Even now, even in hiring practices, you may have someone who has paid their way through and gotten a theology degree and is applying for a position at a parish, and due to finances, they're going to take someone less qualified because they won't have to pay them as much."[5] She saw this as systematically excluding the best-prepared and most committed people from our religious education and ministry programs.

Because of the low pay and limited prospects associated with working for the Catholic Church, there is a willingness to tolerate poor performance in Catholic organizations. One participant with experience working on the local and national levels reported, "There is very much a culture that I've found in most church organizations of being unwilling to confront, in a healthy way, bad behaviors in terms of employment, and just there's a settling for mediocrity, both in clergy and lay [employees]."[6] Another participant in this meeting added, "There's not a willingness to remove someone because they're not competent in their job, and you're also not willing to invest in forming them so they could be competent."[7]

Some of this reluctance to confront employees is due to the idea that the Catholic Church should run differently given its mission. A participant with experience in human resources said,

> We have our HR standards and our evaluations, but we think we have to be nice to people instead of telling them the truth about their performance and what they do. We have a system in place so that if someone is not performing at the level then [certain things should] happen. But because supervisors think they need to be nice to these folks and try to bring them along as opposed to saying you have to stop this and start doing that, we have people carried through for years and years and years.[8]

She described this problem as undermining the morale of hardworking employees. They see someone who is not giving their best effort, but nothing happens.[9]

Others identified the tendency to avoid conflict as the source of the lack of appropriate feedback for church employees. One administrator admitted, "Nobody wants to be the bad guy, so we pass [problems] on to the people whose job it is to name these things."[10] The result is that HR is overwhelmed with basic management issues. Since these HR departments lack staff, there tends to be insufficient follow-through. When they do follow through, he said they simply identify what you did wrong and the consequences for your actions. The result is an unhealthy workplace.

For youth and young adult ministries, we tend to hire young, idealistic Catholics in their early twenties, but according to one participant, most will not last more than two years. He continued, "They are not moving on to be the DRE or to be a campus minister. They are done."[11] He said the same is true with Catholic school teachers, who might last three years. When they leave these positions, he reported that very few return to work for the church in other capacities. If true, we are not building capacity in Catholic education or youth and young adult ministry, which undoubtedly plays a role in the large number of young Catholics who stop participating in community life.

Creating organizations that lack the capacity to meet their objectives is evidence of an organization that has adopted mimicry as the best strategy for responding to its critics. One of the dangers of isomorphic mimics is that they undermine the credibility of an organization when they are exposed. They are frequently the result of a reform that failed due to wishful thinking, which is a failure to plan for the time and resources necessary to effectively implement a reform.

To be clear, we believe that the people who work in youth ministry on the local and national levels are committed to improving how the Catholic Church serves children and young people. The people we interviewed do the best they can with inadequate resources. The situation is better for those working in campus ministry in universities, which designate this as part of the mission. However, one participant said you learn how important mission is in the budget meetings, which suggests our mission offices and programs may also be mimics. An organization that has succumbed to mimicry may do some good, but it will not be able to meet its objectives.

If the Catholic Church paid its employees a living wage, offered training, and provided a better working environment, it would be more likely to retain them. Lower wages and lack of professional advancement cannot simply be endured as some kind of sacrificial offering in service to the mission of the church when an employee's salary and benefits are split among a spouse and children. The Catholic Church cannot excuse itself by saying that people freely accept unjust wages. Pope Leo XIII wrote,

> Now, were we to consider labor merely in so far as it is personal, doubtless it would be within the worker's right to accept any rate of wages whatsoever; for in the same way as a person is free to work or not, so a person is free to accept a small wage or even none at all. But our conclusion must be very different if, together with the personal element in work, we consider the fact that work is also necessary for a person to live: these two aspects of work are separable in thought, but not in reality. The preservation of life is the bounden duty of one and all, and to be wanting therein is a crime.[12]

He declared that when employers pay a less-than-fair wage, the employee is the victim of force and injustice.[13] Paying a living wage and offering on-the-job training would help the church escape the capacity trap and its resulting mimics by retaining better personnel.

As a professor we interviewed put it, there are mimicking structures peppered throughout the Catholic Church as an organization. "I think that is part and parcel of the way the church works, right now," he continued, "and that's painful and disappointing, but that's what it is."[14] He pointed to parish councils and seminary boards as examples, but the list of mimics generated by the people we interviewed was long and included sexual abuse training programs, Co-workers in the Vineyard, the USCCB, human resources and finance departments in Catholic organizations, diocesan review boards, and seminary formation programs. Given the role of seminaries and theologates in selecting, screening, and forming men for holy orders, mimicry in these organizations deserves careful consideration.

SEMINARY FORMATION

Seminaries were established by the Council of Trent as part of a larger Catholic reform movement that sought to provide better formation and education for the clergy. John Olin argued that the reforms to priestly formation Cardinal Ximenes implemented in Toledo after he became the archbishop in 1495 marks the beginning of a coherent and constructive reform movement that predates Luther.[15] Other reformers such as John Colet, Erasmus, and Bishop Matteo Giberti of Verona championed reforming the church by improving the education and formation of young men preparing for priesthood.

Trent institutionalized this aspect of their reform agenda by requiring the establishment of seminaries and their ongoing financial support. As we saw in chapter 2, the focus of Catholic reform was on improving the clergy because people believed that it was the ignorance and corruption of the clergy that were responsible for all of the church's ills. They believed that if they reformed the priests, through a prolonged process of spiritual and intellectual training, the reform of the rest of the church would naturally follow.[16]

The establishment of the seminaries as a means to reform the church proved to be a form of wishful thinking. Having better-educated priests, insofar as that happened, was good; however, Trent recommended expelling seminarians who were incorrigible or spreading bad habits "only when necessary," which may call to mind Jesuit rules concerning dismissing men.[17] The seminaries remained under the control of the bishops; however, it was the bishops who had been ordaining unfit men to the priesthood. Though the council laid out a curriculum, there were no requirements that seminarians pass their courses or meet certain standards for promotion. Since the Catholic Church was not open to innovation in the seminaries and there was no way to measure their performance, mimicry became an optimal strategy for many, if not most, of them.[18]

As higher education became more standardized and accrediting bodies emerged, seminary education in the Catholic Church appeared to become more rigorous as well. The current *Program for Priestly Formation in the United States* (*PPF*) dictates, "Seminaries should have degree programs certified by appropriate accrediting agencies. Seminarians should not be excused from pursuing such degrees except for serious reasons. A seminarian is normally expected to obtain the master of divinity and/or the STB degree prior to ordination."[19] In the United States the minimum number of credits for a master of divinity degree set by the Association of Theological Schools is seventy-two semester credits. Most Catholic seminaries have over one hundred credits associated with their master of divinity degrees.

The problem is that any statements prefaced by "should," "ought," "should not," or "ought not" can be dispensed with by a bishop or religious superior.[20] As a member of the Apostolic Visitation of Seminaries in the wake of the *Boston Globe* reporting on sexual abuse, Anderson learned from the faculty that there were seminarians who failed every class but still moved forward. When he checked their academic records, he found they were not enrolled in programs, and consequently were invisible to accrediting agencies. Men were being ordained without degrees.

Bishops, Anderson learned, were only bound by statements prefaced by "must." If you were to go through the *PPF* and highlight all the norms prefaced by "should" or "ought," the mimicry becomes apparent.[21] Seminaries Anderson visited did psychological evaluations, but admitted men that their psychologist found to be unstable. Some seminaries admitted men who did not understand the language of instruction, did not have high school degrees, admitted recent drug use, and were actively addicted to pornography—all of whom the *PPF* said should not be admitted.

To be clear, most seminarians at these seminaries met the standards and were enrolled in programs. We should also recognize that the seminary faculty noted and recorded the problems. Yet since almost all of this information is compartmentalized and kept confidential, very few seminary faculty members were aware of some, if any, of these issues. And bishops can and do intervene to override concerns.

The report on the Apostolic Visitation, which was released in 2008, presented a very positive assessment of the U.S. seminaries. Most of the criticisms focused on the presence of a small number of faculty, "even in the best seminaries," who expressed reservations about some magisterial teachings. The report criticized seminaries that allowed laypeople to vote on the worthiness of candidates and forbade the practice. After reporting that the Visitors almost universally judged the admissions criteria positively, it recognized some of the problems the Visitation revealed in the most general terms possible, stating,

> Worrisome were the cases where seminaries have been pressured to accept obviously unsuitable candidates, or to unduly abbreviate a candidate's course of formation, to hurry him on to ordination. Clearly, in some places, lack of vocations has caused some lowering of standards. Such a strategy risks possible wretched consequences. Seminary rectors, in conscience, must always keep the barriers to ordination high.[22]

This potentially alarming statement was immediately followed by the reassurance that the character of candidates was almost universally praised by the Visitors. From our perspective, this reveals that the Visitation was a mimic. It produced no details of how many unsuitable candidates were accepted, why they were unsuitable, and what seminaries were involved. In short, the report accentuated the positive and produced no action plan to eliminate the negative.

When we explained mimicry during our interviews and how informal rules can undermine formal rules to the people engaged in priestly formation, participants revealed that they had encountered mimicry in their work. A member of a formation team said that the human and spiritual formation that is supposed to take place does not happen: "The accountability piece, the hard words, [the] challenges that need to be stated are very infrequently stated in those contexts."[23] By now, such conflict avoidance is quite familiar, but this professor also explained that formation faculty tend to identify silence and a reticence to speak as a sign of holiness, which allows candidates for the priesthood to hide issues they need to confront. Another person we interviewed said that religious orders sometimes ask that their men take a less demanding degree than the master of divinity. Yet another pointed out how many of the academic policies in their program are prefaced with words such as *normally*, which signals that the policy is not required.

While it is typical for academic programs to have some room for exceptions in their admissions and academic policies, the degree of latitude is much more restricted for professional programs. Medical schools do not, for example, grant students who cannot pass their curriculum a master's in biology and allow them to practice medicine. We also expect medical doctors to have passed their courses as well as exams by independent medical boards to certify their competence. Professionals who are trained to work with vulnerable people have to meet rigorous standards in other fields; however, medical doctors, mental health professionals, and social workers do not claim to be configured to Christ and to serve as "visible signs of the merciful love of the Father in the Church and the world."[24] The ideology that a priest is configured to Christ regardless of his knowledge or moral formation is at the heart of magisterial documents that govern seminary formation.

SEEDBEDS OF CLERICALISM

Organizations and societies stuck on unproductive paths reinforce their course by shaping the learning process. Douglass North argued that the most decisive factor in an organization's development is how it shapes the direction of knowledge and skills. Seminary education in the Catholic Church is governed on the international level by the Congregation for the Clergy that produces the *Ratio Fundamentalis Instructionis Sacerdotalis* (*Ratio*). The *Ratio* is then used to create the *PPF*. Though the *Ratio* states that priests should be educated so that "they do not become prey to 'clericalism,'" it promotes an idealized vision not only of priests but also of seminarians.[25]

The *PPF* provides an excellent example of how the church reinforces the ideology of clericalism. The document dictates, "All priestly formation must have its foundation in an adherence to the truths of faith about the nature and mission of the ministerial priesthood. Members of the seminary community who are involved in the process of priestly formation must adhere to these teachings."[26] When one checks the notes, it becomes clear that sources for the truths of the ministerial priesthood are essentially drawn from two twentieth-century sources: Vatican II and *Pastores Dabo Vobis*.

Pastores Dabo Vobis is an apostolic exhortation promulgated by Pope John Paul II in 1992 after the Synod of Bishops. The document presents an idealized model of priesthood and formation in order to call for reform. Like other ideal models we have seen in church history, it soon came to be seen as definitive of priesthood rather than something priests should strive to attain. Our concern is not so much with *Pastores Dabo Vobis* as it is with how church leaders have used the document to reinforce clericalism in the current editions of the *Ratio* and *PPF*. The *PPF* virtually identifies the truths of faith about the ministerial priesthood with Pope John Paul II's exhortation.

The *Ratio* defines the purpose of formation as developing a priestly identity. A priestly vocation "begins with a gift of divine grace, which is then sealed in sacramental ordination."[27] A priest is configured to Christ from "the first moment of his calling."[28] The gradual configuration to Christ "*causes* the sentiments and attitudes of the Son of God to arise in the life of the disciple."[29] The *Ratio* does not explain how someone already configured to Christ becomes gradually more configured over time. The seminarian is called "to a basic human and spiritual serenity that, by overcoming every form of self-promotion or emotional dependency, allows him to be a man of communion and dialogue."[30]

Seminarians are assisted in achieving this remarkable state, according to the *Ratio*, by their intimate relationship with the Lord and by fraternal communion. Seminarians "recognize and correct 'spiritual worldliness,' obsession with personal appearances, a presumed theological or disciplinary certainty, narcissism and authoritarianism, the attempt to dominate others, and every form of careerism."[31] With God's grace, the future priest learns "how to interpret and understand his own motivations, his gifts, his needs and frailties, so as 'to free himself from all disordered affections and having removed them, to seek out and find the will of God in the ordering of his life with a view to the salvation of the soul.'"[32] The *Ratio* quotes Ignatius of Loyola as its source.

Integral formation, the *Ratio* explains, is of the greatest importance "because the whole person, with all that he is and all that he possesses, who will be at the Lord's service in the Christian community."[33] The people called to the priesthood are not like other people; instead, men called to the priesthood are defined as "integral subjects." Integral subjects, unlike the rest of humanity, are those "who have previously chosen to attain a sound interior life, without divisions or contradictions."[34] These men must be exceptional to meet the requirement for ordination, which the *Ratio* described this way:

> Priestly ordination ***requires***, in the one who receives it, a complete giving of himself for the service of the People of God, as an image of Christ the Spouse....Thus, he is ***required*** to "be capable of loving people with a heart which

is new, generous, and pure—with genuine self-detachment, with full, constant and faithful dedication and at the same time with a kind of 'divine jealousy' (cf. 2 Cor. 11:2) and even with a kind of maternal tenderness."[35] (emphasis ours)

The document is quoting from John Paul II's exhortation, but it has taken an ideal and established it as a standard for ordination. If this is the requirement for ordination, who meets it? While we affirm that there are many good and faithful priests, we have not met any that could meet this standard, which seems unattainable except perhaps for a handful of saints. At this point, the document moves from wishful to magical thinking.

It is the priests' perfect detachment and purity of heart that justifies their authority to govern. The *Ratio* connects detachment and governance:

> The call to be pastors of the People of God requires a formation that makes future priests experts in the art of pastoral discernment, that is to say, able to listen deeply to real situations and capable of good judgment in making choices and decisions....In listening closely, respectfully and without prejudice, the pastor becomes able to read the lives of others without being superficial or judgmental. He enters into the heart of the person and into the contexts of life that distinguish him, above all into the internal and external obstacles that can, at times, produce problematic behavior. He will be able to interpret with wisdom and understanding all kinds of things that condition people and influence their lives.[36]

Priests are men of discernment who are able to "read the reality of human life in the light of the Spirit" and "are able to choose, decide, and act according to the will of God."[37]

St. Catherine of Siena taught her disciples that the attempt to read other people's intentions is simply a projection of the self on others, but our seminarians are being formed to think that they can read people's intentions with the aid of the Holy Spirit. Catherine, who is a doctor of the church, wrote that Christians, a category that includes priests, are "to discern My [God's] will rather than judge other people's intentions."[38] From the standpoint of Catholic spirituality, the claim to be able to read people's lives and intentions is presumption pure and simple. It is easy to see how this idea could foster a sense of elitism and superiority not to mention how it would reinforce narcissistic tendencies. There are a host of theological problems with these documents as they are being used, which fall outside of the scope of this project, but there are two significant theological problems that must be named: The first is related to history and the second is related to defined doctrine on sin.

In Catholic theology, history can be understood as indicating the content of Christian religion. Hugh of St. Victor, who wrote the first *summa*, taught that the religion of Christ is not based on logic but on a series of facts arranged in a history. Hugh was inspired by St. Augustine, who was so concerned with history that he wrote *The City of God*. Catholic theology is replete with theologians, saints, and doctors who have affirmed the revelatory nature of history. Vatican II emphasized the importance of "reading the signs of the times."[39]

Knowing history and striving for fidelity to the facts are essential for good theology. Does the portrait of the priest promoted by the Congregation for the Clergy reflect how priests have acted throughout church history? If not, is the Congregation claiming that ordination today is superior to ordination in the past? It appears that either they do not care about fidelity to the facts, or they are completely ignorant of church history.

We can also think of history in terms of our personal experiences in the past and the present. How many priests and bishops have you known? How many meet the requirement for ordination presented in the *Ratio*? If you do not really know any priests or bishops well, you still know about the sexual abuse scandal. Did the priests and bishops act in ways that confirm priests and bishops know the will of God and act upon it? A valid theology of priesthood and holy orders should be as consonant with your experience as it is with church history.

One thing is certain, the idealized image of the priest is not what we find in church history. The early church did not idealize priests or even apostles. The New Testament frequently points out the flaws of St. Peter and other apostles such as the sons of Zebedee. Before the crucifixion, Peter denied Christ three times, and after Pentecost, Peter made a mistake over dietary issues in Acts and was rebuked by St. Paul.

Citing Hosea 5:1, "Bad priests are a snare of ruin for my people," Gregory the Great advised people to learn how to discern between good and bad priests to avoid being spiritually destroyed.[40] He warned the ordained to avoid the trap of seeing the power of their rank in themselves. Instead, he taught that pastors should focus on the equality of their nature with the people they serve. Rather than concentrating on ordination as a source of authority, Gregory grounded Christian authority on service.[41] Yet another doctor of the church, Bernard of Clairvaux, warned of Judas priests and called for them to reform: "Woe to the unfaithful stewards who, themselves not yet reconciled [to God], take on the responsibility of recognizing righteousness in others, as if they were themselves righteous men." Bernard called them "vessels fit for destruction" (Rom 9:22).[42]

The reform decrees of the ecumenical councils also indicate that perfect self-detachment and purity of heart are neither a requirement for ordination nor caused by it. Though there are many examples of such decrees, the Decree on Reform from the Fourteenth Session of Trent should be sufficient to make the point:

> Since it is properly the office of bishops to reprove the faults of their subjects, they must take particular care not to acquiesce if clerics, especially those appointed to the pastoral care of souls, are guilty of leading unworthy lives. For if they pass over irregular and corrupt practices, how can they rebuke the laity for their vices when they could be confounded by one word from the latter for permitting clerics to be much worse than they? And how free will priests be to correct the laity, when they can quietly answer that the priests have themselves behaved in the very way they are reproving?[43]

Trent presents priests as human beings who struggle with vice and sin. Yet, the *Ratio* suggests that this could not be a problem since all priests are integral people due to their calling. If the *Ratio* is right about the identity of the priest, there would not have been a Protestant Reformation. If priests do not have disordered passions, how can we explain a worldwide clergy sexual abuse scandal?

The doctrinal problem is that the *Ratio* and, therefore, the *PPF* seem to be at variance with the defined doctrines related to original sin. Can someone sin who has overcome every form of self-promotion or emotional dependency, removed all of their disordered affections, attained genuine self-detachment, and lives with full, constant, and faithful dedication? It would seem that such people would not suffer from concupiscence, which is defined as the tendency to sin. Trent declared, as defined doctrine, that baptism removes the guilt of original sin but that concupiscence or the tendency to sin remains in everyone. Everyone is a category that includes priests. The only exception to having original sin and concupiscence other than Jesus, according to Trent, is "the blessed and immaculate virgin Mary, mother of God."[44] Trent anathematized anyone who contradicted that we all suffer from the tendency to sin.

Catholic doctrine is clear that everyone is afflicted by sin and concupiscence, which is not sin itself but leads to sin. Chapter Ten of Trent's Declaration on Justification states, "For in this mortal life men and women, however holy and just, will sometimes fall into sin, at least light and everyday sins which are also called venial, but they do not therefore cease to be just. For the voice that says, *Forgive us our trespasses*, is the voice of the just and it is humble and truthful."[45] Trent advises,

> And because we all make many mistakes, each of us ought to keep before his eyes the severity and judgment as much as the mercy and goodness; and even if he is not aware of anything in himself, a person ought not to pronounce judgment on himself, for our whole life must be examined and judged not by our judgment but by that of God, *who will bring to light the things now hidden in darkness and discloses the purposes of the heart.*[46]

If the *Ratio* does not formally contradict the letter of Trent, it certainly contradicts its spirit.

Catholic doctrine calls us to humility. The beauty of humility is that it allows people to be merciful with themselves and others. At the same time, humility forces us to recognize that we can be better. Holiness is an open-ended horizon because we can always be more faithful, hopeful, and loving. It is not an identity given at ordination. More importantly, the doctrine that we all sin, we all make mistakes, and we all need to strive to be better with the help of God's grace is so much more humane than the ideology of clericalism promoted in our seminaries.

The idealized portrait of the priest and of the seminarian creates tremendous cognitive dissonance for the men entering seminaries as well as for those who are ordained. One thing that a man who spends more than a year in the seminary learns is that he and his classmates do not possess human and spiritual serenity, freedom from spiritual worldliness, or the purity of heart that comes from eradicating all disordered passions. He also sees that priests on the faculty are sometimes driven by careerism, or have problems with drinking, or suffer from pride and vanity. This is not to say that the seminarians and their faculty are terrible people; rather, it is to affirm that they are people.

It is unhealthy to live with so much cognitive dissonance. By the time a man has been ordained, he has learned that maintaining his reputation as a man who acts with constant and full devotion is critical for justifying his authority. He has also learned that he needs to protect priestly identity in general, which requires charitable discretion when it comes to the behavior of other priests. When he is done, he will know the informal rules of the game related to patronage and accept them as normal. He may recognize some of the problems that emerge when a bishop or superior reveals a lack of judgment or virtue, but he is more likely to try to mitigate the problems than to confront leadership or publicize failures to the people of God.

Rather than support priestly authority, these claims to perfection have led many people to the conclusion that the priesthood—and by extension the church—is a mimic. When the distance between what people have been taught concerning who a priest is according to magisterial documents and their experience or knowledge of how priests actually behave cannot be reconciled, the church loses its credibility. A church without credibility has nothing to offer, so people leave. As they leave, we lose our capacity to help the poor, to teach, to reconcile divisions, and engage in all aspects of building the kingdom of God.

We cannot conclude this section without emphasizing that the *Ratio* we have been discussing was published in 2016, which is more than a decade after the clerical abuse scandal erupted in the United States. It was also written after the clergy abuse scandals in the Philippines (2002), Ireland (2005), Germany (2010), Netherlands (2011), Australia (2013), and Poland (2013). Unfortunately, this is not a comprehensive list. The *Ratio* was published two years after the United Nations publicly condemned the Vatican's response to clergy sexual abuse of children. Surely the members of the Congregation for the Clergy were aware of these events when they drafted and approved the document. Rather than face problems with priestly formation, the Congregation for the Clergy retreated into a fantasy with little connection to reality.

The sad reality is that as scandals have erupted, Rome has responded by leaning into the rhetoric of priestly perfection. There have been two previous editions of the *Ratio*. The first was promulgated in

1970 and the second in 1985. The two earlier editions are quite similar, so we will focus on the 1970 *Ratio* for the sake of simplicity.

The purpose of formation, according to the earlier versions, is the perfection of charity, which should lead the student to become "in a special way another Christ so that 'he should truly recognize what he is doing when he celebrates the mystery of Christ's death.'" The earlier editions contextualize being *alter Christus* in the context of the liturgy.[47] They do not claim that the priest is *alter Christus* in all aspects of their lives. The priest is ordained so that he can take on the role of Christ in the liturgy.

The 1970 edition of the *Ratio* emphasized that imitating Christ, who came to serve rather than be served, means priests should see themselves in terms of service. It presented the role of the spiritual director in assisting students to develop virtues. The students "should endeavor to bring the grace of their baptism to perfection." Moreover, students should develop an ever clearer and more definite appreciation of their special priestly vocation, and so make themselves better able to acquire the virtues and habits of priestly life."[48] The priest has a vocation rather than an identity and the seminarian is not someone who has "from the first moment of his calling" become configured to Christ as an integral person.

The 1970 *Ratio* did not describe seminarians as being configured to Christ; instead, it states,

> The student should aim at a close and friendly relationship with the person and mission of Christ, who completed His task (cf Jn. 4:34) in humble submission to the will of the Father. This relationship of necessity demands that a candidate for the priesthood should know how to "dedicate his own will, by obedience, to the service of God and his brethren," with sincere faith. One who wishes to have a part with Christ crucified in the building up of His Body is under a grave obligation not only to learn to accept the cross, but also to love it, and to take up in a willing and pastoral spirit all the heavy tasks required to carry on his apostolic mission.[49]

The superiors, according to the earlier editions, should train the men to rely upon and be obedient to Christ. The change from teaching seminarians that they should aim for a close and friendly relationship with Christ to teaching seminarians to see themselves as so configured to

Christ that it causes "the sentiments and attitudes of the Son of God to arise" in their lives is clear evidence of increasing clericalism in the Catholic Church.[50]

The earlier editions of the *Ratio* present a more modest and humble understanding of priesthood. They did not describe priests as possessing perfect detachment, as being able to read other people's lives, or as both knowing and doing the will of God. Instead, the earlier editions describe priesthood this way: "In virtue of the sacrament of order, they are consecrated in the likeness of Christ, high and eternal priest (cf. Heb. 5:1–10; 7:24; 9:11–28), as genuine priests of the New Testament, for the work of preaching the gospel, tending the faithful, and celebrating divine worship."[51]

The new edition of the *Ratio* will exacerbate the problems stemming from clericalism. By setting forth standards that no one can meet, men applying to and enrolled in seminaries are less likely to freely communicate their struggles to formators. Seminary faculty, deans, and rectors will not be able to use these idealized standards to determine who should move forward and who should not. Having standards or norms that cannot be enforced will further undermine discipline. Ask yourself, "Will men who are formed to see themselves as configured to Christ since they felt called to priesthood consider themselves as subject to the same laws and norms as everyone else?"

CONCLUSION

The new *Ratio* has, to borrow a common phrase, doubled down on the idealization of the priest to justify clerical authority. It explicitly locates power in the integral person of the ordained priest who is configured to Christ, thereby reinforcing the power differentials that discourage victims from reporting their assailants. Worse, it continues to provide an incentive to conceal or at least minimize the crimes of priests. It instills a spirit of exceptionalism as the seminarian learns that the standards, such as mastery of his courses, do not really apply to him. What really matters is having a bishop or superior who will support you and ordain you.

The more priests are idealized, the less a priest can be assessed. Once the ideal is established as a standard, however, mimicry becomes the only workable strategy. The way to succeed as a seminarian is to project a "priestly identity" by revealing as little as possible. If they engage in fraternal correction, they learn that doing so will invite others to point out their faults. They come to recognize fraternal correction as a type of mimic and to embrace the incentives to practice "charitable discretion" when they speak. The discrepancy between the idealized standard and reality is explained in terms of pastoral concerns such as mercy and forgiveness. The seminarians learn that the informal rules, particularly those related to patronage and maintaining the reputation of priests, matter much more than written standards and policies.

The men formed in this system will bring their understanding of priestly identity and patronage into the dioceses, schools, and other settings where they are given administrative posts. Priests are placed in management roles without the requisite training and experience to perform well. For example, a priest might direct or manage a school even though he has no training in education. He would most likely hire inexpensive and inexperienced applicants as administrators and teachers. Young and inexperienced people are less likely to challenge the priest's decisions. Since the priest did not receive special or ongoing training for his new position, he is not likely to support such training for his subordinates unless it is mandated.

Lay employees quickly learn that power is personal and that their positions rely on patronage rather than performance. There are no metrics to evaluate the priest in charge and it becomes clear to the other employees that the organization has low expectations. The employees who do an excellent job come to recognize that there are no consequences for poor performance, no rewards for good performance, and no hopes for advancement. As a result, most of the talented and committed Catholics who work for Catholic organizations leave as soon as they can find a better opportunity. Because we are so focused on priests, Catholics do not recognize the extent of the damage caused by this constant turnover.

Clericalism creates a culture that combines exceptionalism with low expectations. This culture is unhealthy for all of us. It distorts the process of screening, forming, and approving men for ordination. Clericalism also impedes the selection, training, and retention of talented lay employees that Catholic organizations need to thrive. The problems mirror each other because both priests and lay employees work within an organization that relies on patronage, with its inherent power differentials, maintains a culture of silence, and is replete with unwritten rules and ways of proceeding.

Changing the rules of the game, the institutions, generated by clericalism cannot be solved using top-down or universal solutions from the Vatican; however, we cannot begin the process of finding solutions without changes to canon law that would allow for the experimentation necessary to find solutions. We also need the Vatican to reconsider the current *Ratio*, whether there should be a universal document governing priestly formation, and how such a document is created. Only the Vatican has the authority to root out all the idealized descriptions of priests contained in documents like *The Catechism of the Catholic Church*. Nonetheless, implementing sustainable reforms requires us to enter into a process of finding solutions at the lowest and most local level possible. In the conclusion, we will discuss the steps necessary to implement the institutional reforms we need.

CONCLUSION

Bernard of Clairvaux wrote that people who complain about evil without considering how to remedy it or identifying what is good are mere detractors rather than reformers.[1] We certainly wish to avoid being detractors. We acknowledge the tremendous role the Catholic Church has played in our lives, and we know that there are many other people on the margins that the church lifts up, teaches, and defends. We have not been using the term *church* to designate the clergy alone. Without the financial support, service, and work of the laity, the Catholic Church could not maintain itself as an organization. In fact, the laity possesses a type of primacy because the clergy quite literally come from the laity insofar as all priests have mothers, who—of course—were not ordained.

Our commitment to the Catholic Church requires us to call attention to the fact that our community remains caught in the perilous dynamic created by the ideology of clericalism. With each new report of a bishop's or religious superior's failure to protect people from a sexual predator, the Catholic Church loses more credibility. If the current formal and informal rules or institutions remain in place, then changes in leadership and revisions to the Code of Canon Law will not produce sustainable reforms by themselves. Changing the rules that promote silence and that deny the laity's role in holding the clergy accountable will be necessary to break path dependency.

Institutional reform is entangled with other types of reform in the Catholic Church. Structural reforms related to governance and administration are also necessary. We need to change how we select and train candidates for holy orders. Magisterial teachings that create insurmountable power differentials between clergy and laity must be excised from sources like catechisms and catechetical programs. Institutional reform requires all of us to bring our expertise and experience to bear on the problem of sexual abuse as a community of faith. Without uprooting the rules that create favorable conditions for sexual abuse and its concealment, the church cannot maintain its flock, much less evangelize.

The ordained play a particular role in the mission of the church, which is important, but their role includes acknowledging the ministries and charisms that the laity brings for the sanctification of the world. Ordained ministry is not personal; instead, it is a public form of service to a community. The claim that ministry is a possession or a personal privilege that exempts priests and bishops from accountability to the people they serve asserts rights and privileges over and against the common good.

Given that priests and bishops offer a public form of service, they must be assessed and evaluated by the communities they serve in a clear and transparent manner. Metrics should be established that prioritize the concerns of the laity in the parishes, dioceses, and religious provinces that priests serve. Church employees should be included in the assessment process and the creation of metrics because they are frequently the most informed members of the community in terms of the performance of priests, bishops, and religious superiors. In short, we should implement periodic 360-degree reviews in all of the church's organizations. The information generated by such assessments must be shared and play a substantial role in all personnel decisions regarding ordained clergy.

Vatican II declared that the laity had a "special task to shed light upon and order all temporal matters in which they are closely involved."[2] This includes the temporal matters of the church. As people who are closely involved with the temporal matters of the church, we have taken up our special task by shedding light on clericalism and its institutional effects. Now that the trap is visible, it's possible for us to deconstruct it; however, the process will be neither easy nor fast.

The single most important thing to understand about implementing institutional reform is that it is by nature incremental and iterative.[3] We must keep at it. This is because the rules, norms, and beliefs that we have inherited are deeply embedded and are difficult to change. As we have seen, efforts to implement reform from the top down, such as the Dallas Charter or *Vos Estis Lux Mundi*, will most likely result in mimicry, wishful thinking, and premature load bearing. Continuous incremental change will only come about when the rules of the game and the institutions provide a framework for evolutionary change.[4] There is an analog to an evolutionary framework in Catholic theology and doctrine: the sense of the faithful. The sense of the faithful emerges from a process of communal discernment involving the whole church; however, secrecy and silence over criminal behavior prevent the church from bringing the sense of the faithful to bear on the problems.

Vatican II encouraged the laity to be actively involved in the church and to exercise their prophetic role, which requires that the laity know about the failures of ecclesial leaders. Hiding these problems impedes our ability to learn as a community.[5] In his magisterial book on the sense of the faithful, John Burkhard, OFM Conv., wrote, "If more Catholics believed that their engagement was welcome in the church, I submit that the scandals rocking the church today would be less an occasion for leaving the church and more an incentive for all believers to tackle these problems."[6] The sense of the faithful is a dynamic reality manifested in consensus, which only occurs when the laity and clergy agree on a doctrinal matter.[7] If such consensus is required for doctrinal matters, including definitions of faith, then how can we deny that there should be consensus on disciplinary matters and governance?

Rooting out clericalism and changing the rules of the game that foster sexual abuse and its concealment requires an integrated, three-pronged response. The first is to reject the apologetics of perfection, which requires a change to the narrative for our *nomos* or "the normative universe where we create and maintain our sense of right and wrong, of lawful and unlawful, of valid and void."[8] The second is to recover and promote a more inclusive and dynamic understanding of hierarchy found in the early church. The third is to root out the rules, the unconscious habits, which serve to conceal the crimes and failures of priests and laity who betray the more vulnerable members of our communion.

INSTITUTIONAL REFORM

Changing the formal and informal institutions guiding decisions will require many small alterations in the rules between and among the clergy and laity.[9] Such a process, which impinges on matters of power and authority, will generate conflict. As we have seen, Catholics tend to avoid both personal and public conflict within the church. One source for this aversion is the emphasis on unity as one of the identifying marks of the church, but another source is the attempt to preserve the appearance of perfection.

Yet conflict is not a sign of imperfection or a lack of holiness. There were many conflicts in the apostolic church as evidenced by the Acts of the Apostles and the Pauline Epistles. Later, there were conflicts over the books that would be included in the biblical canon, the Trinity, and Christology. As we have seen, there have been conflicts between Catholic civil and religious authorities throughout history. Do these conflicts indicate that the church was not holy? If we adopt John Henry Newman's definition of *perfection*, we will see conflict as an indication of the Catholic Church's vitality. "In a higher world it is otherwise," Newman wrote, "but here below to live is to change, and to be perfect is to have changed often."[10] Perfection is the ability to adapt to new contexts without losing identity, and such adaptation necessarily entails conflict.

Given our aversion to conflict, we need to create frameworks or structures to hold and mediate tensions over governance on the local level. If we fail to do so, we will continue to incentivize people to organize dissent, create parties, and exit the Catholic Church.[11] While the exact nature and number of these structures would need to be adapted to local contexts, they must include the establishment of third-party accountability organizations composed of local people who reflect the community. Because the rules and the incentives that foster sexual abuse and its concealment are embedded in how we approach discipline and accountability at large, the scope of their work must extend beyond the narrow confines of sexual abuse.

These accountability organizations must be independent of the local bishop or superior, but they should include priests who can serve as bridges to the bishop or religious superior. Certainly, they would need to be authorized to do their work by bishops and religious superiors. This may require some changes to canon law; however, given the sweeping discretion bishops possess when it comes to church law, there may be steps they can implement immediately. Church history provides precedents for such accountability organizations. For example, Gregory the Great established the *defensores*, who were not ordained, with the rights and privileges necessary to investigate the crimes of the clergy.[12] As late as 1064, Peter Damian encouraged Duchess Adelaide of Turin to investigate abuses and punish even the most preeminent members of the clergy in her territory.[13]

While the third-party accountability groups would not have the authority to punish priests, they would need the authority to audit their diocese's or province's files concerning disciplinary matters, including priest personnel and seminary files. They would be charged with publicizing any violations of civil and canon law as well as problems they find regarding policies and procedures that serve to undermine proper discipline. In this way, their findings could be aggregated, analyzed, and shared so that we can learn from our successes and failures.

Providing transparency around decisions involving sexual abuse in Catholic dioceses and religious orders is a necessary step for restoring credibility, but it is not sufficient to break the cycle of wishful thinking, mimicry, and premature load bearing. Economists have shown that "problem driven iterative adaptation" is the best way for organizations to escape capability traps.[14] They argue that identifying the problems and finding solutions on the local level are more effective than trying to find a universal solution or best practice to implement.

Local people's involvement helps build organizational capacity—the organization's ability to fulfill its mission or purpose. In the process, people come to recognize and assess the weaknesses of existing structures and processes. Members of these accountability groups begin to learn the formal and informal rules that need to be deinstitutionalized. As agents across the system become aware of weaknesses, they build multinetwork coalitions to deal with common concerns.[15] Once people are aware of the various challenges, they are less susceptible to wishful thinking.

Finally, successful accountability organizations are encouraged to experiment. Experimentation is important because the pressure to embrace mimicry increases when the space for innovation is closed. Centralized and top-down approaches emphasize compliance whereas locally defined problems and solutions emphasize performance. The emphasis on performance leads these groups to establish metrics to discern what is successful, what is not, and why. Rather than trying to craft a perfect solution, they take an iterative approach that continually seeks better ways of doing things.[16]

Adopting this problem-solving approach to institutional reform is consistent with the Catholic principle of subsidiarity, and it would begin to shift colloquial discourse about the church from them, meaning the bishops, to us. Inviting people to examine problems would inoculate them against an idealized understanding of the church, which sets people up for scandal when they encounter the wounded church. More modest expectations diminish the likelihood of premature load bearing and its attendant erosion of credibility.

Creating metrics and enforcement mechanisms would serve to

diminish the power differentials that discourage people from reporting abuse. Informing those who reported abuse of the actions taken as a result would remove another disincentive for reporting. When bishops, superiors, or rectors minimize red flags related to sexual abuse, their actions should be publicized to the diocese or province. If they hide crimes, these accountability groups would report the matter to law enforcement for criminal prosecution. In this way, these groups would help the clergy learn how to discern between what is sinful, what is criminal, and what is both.

There is also a pressing need to reform a host of "consultative mimics" in the church, beginning with the seminaries. Seminary faculty as a whole must have more than a consultative role in determining whether someone is ordained. Seminary boards need deliberative power as well as the right to regularly and independently audit the seminaries to ensure compliance with standards. The Fourth Lateran Council recommended that bishops who promote unsuitable men to church offices be stripped of that power, but perhaps it is time to consider measures to prevent such abuses rather than react to them after the fact.[17] Some limitations of episcopal discretion as to who to ordain would provide the additional benefit of greatly diminishing the role of patronage in who is ordained and promoted. Such limits would make it more difficult for predators like former Cardinal McCarrick to abuse seminarians.

Investing parish councils with deliberative power regarding finances and other temporal matters is arguably the second most pressing reform needed to address the problems of power differentials and patronage that prevent people from reporting abuse. The Australian Royal Commission into Institutional Child Abuse showed that people are less likely to report abuse in hierarchical organizations where everyone reports to one person, which is precisely how our parishes and dioceses are structured. Changing the rules of the game will require changes at the local level to establish new institutional norms, but it also demands that we reconsider what we mean when we speak of hierarchy.

THE PROBLEM WITH HIERARCHY

Hierarchy is a term that has almost completely lost its initial meaning. Most people think of hierarchy in terms of an organizational structure because the word has taken on different meanings over time. *Hierarchy* evokes the image of a pyramid where power is concentrated at the top. People typically refer to corporations and military organizations as hierarchies; however, the term's origin is theological. Pseudo-Dionysius the Areopagite, whom we will call Denys, coined the term *hierarchy.* Whereas medieval people believed Denys was a disciple of St. Paul, granting his writings the status of apostolic tradition, we know he was most likely a Syrian monk writing sometime in the late fifth or early sixth century. The original meaning of *hierarchy* is worth considering.[18]

Hierarchy was not about organizational structure for Denys. He defined hierarchy this way: "In my opinion a hierarchy is a sacred order, a state of understanding and an activity approximating as closely as possible to the divine."[19] Hierarchy was understood as a dynamic reality rather than as a static structure. The goal of every hierarchy, according to Denys, is to empower beings to be as like God as possible and to be one with God.

Denys conceived of hierarchy as a liberating and inclusive reality. He included bishops, priests, deacons, religious, the baptized, and catechumens in the ecclesiastical hierarchy.[20] Finally, Denys wrote that hierarchy ensures that its members who have received the divine splendor can then pass on this light generously and in accordance with God's will to those beings who are further down the scale. In short, hierarchy was understood as a relational form of service.

Perfection for every member of the hierarchy, Denys explained, is to be uplifted to imitate God as far as possible and to become what scripture calls a "co-worker for God" (1 Thess 3:2; 1 Cor 3:9; Rom 16:3).[21] Hierarchy is better understood as pointing to sacramental or spiritual values than to juridical or institutional norms. The identifying characteristic of hierarchy, as it was originally conceived, was the function to lift up the lowest member. In that sense, hierarchy is "upliftingly stooped," which means Denys conceived of it in terms of bending down to help pick someone up.[22] This coming down to lift up is an ecclesial form of imitating the Son's self-emptying kenosis.

By restricting the hierarchy to the ordained, particularly to the bishops, we have abandoned its trinitarian foundations; instead, the magisterium has embraced a subordinationist model for its understanding of the church.[23] Of course, the subordination of the laity was Pope Gregory VII's goal when he promoted the liberty of the church. Gregory VII proposed the idea that the ordained clergy should be seen as superior and, therefore, could not be held accountable for their actions by the laity. While superiority and holiness can coexist with perfection in the higher realm, to borrow from Newman, our experience is that leadership requires accountability in the temporal world where people frequently fail to act as they should.

Perhaps the most important idea that we could retrieve from Denys is that the church, the ecclesiastical hierarchy, is not perfect. Bonaventure, commenting on hierarchy, compared the heavenly hierarchy to the sun because it has no darkness in it, but he said the ecclesiastical hierarchy is like the moon because it waxes and wanes in its holiness.[24] Rather than point to perfection, Bonaventure drew upon an older tradition that linked the church's authority to its humility. The Franciscan movement, of course, called the church to embrace the path of penance, which requires a humble admission of faults and a commitment to change.

CHANGING THE NARRATIVE

Reconnecting authority to humility, which is necessary for dismantling the clericalism trap, requires a change to our narrative. The apologetics of perfection promoted by Gregory VII gradually supplanted a more modest understanding of priesthood promoted by the doctors of the church from the fourth until the late eleventh century. This more modest understanding, the apologetics of humility, sought to explain how an imperfect church can lead people to salvation. The apologetics of perfection, on the other hand, had to maintain the perfection of the church in the face of its obvious faults.

In its original form, the apologetics of perfection was grounded in the forms of pastoral ministry provided by the priests. The argument was not that priests were perfect, but that pastoral ministry was superior to all other forms of service. Since this form of service is superior, they argued, only members of the clerical order are competent to judge the actions of the clergy. The apologetic also stressed that clergy should be holy in order to encourage them to voluntarily embrace celibacy and to separate themselves from the affairs of the world. If the leaders were more holy, they reasoned, the whole community would be better.

Unfortunately, the apologetics of perfection was a manifestation of wishful thinking. It is much more difficult to enforce discipline than it is to exhort people to conversion. Enforcement requires personnel with the requisite training to investigate problems and the budgets to do so. Calling for conversion, on the other hand, demands nothing.

There was another flaw with the apologetics of perfection—everyone knew that the clergy were neither ritually pure nor particularly holy. What emerged from the apologetics of perfection was an ecclesial embrace of isomorphic mimicry. Rather than being a holy and perfect order in society, the clergy learned that projecting an image of perfection and holiness would suffice to secure their authority and independence.

Protecting the reputation of priests and bishops—really the entire organization—became vitally important for the clergy to maintain their power and privileges. Since the late Middle Ages, bishops pointed to their role in providing pastoral care to justify their concealment of the crimes of priestly perpetrators. Many in the church came to accept the crimes of priests as the actions of a few bad actors and failed to consider if structural problems or conflicts of interest influenced decision-making.

The ideology that priests are set apart from and placed over the laity, due to their holiness, obscured people's ability to recognize behaviors that would normally provoke suspicion. As exceptional people, priests were allowed to have some eccentricities. Expectations of holiness fed into confirmation bias, which is the tendency to interpret experiences to fit beliefs. These beliefs concerning priestly holiness also create tremendous power differentials, which was the goal of the apologetics of perfection. In this way, clericalism provides camouflage for the predator, discourages victims from reporting, and incentivizes concealment.

As we have seen, clericalism generates a myriad of rules. Priests have to be treated differently and should not be held to the same standards as everyone else. Discipline in the church should proceed by fraternal correction. The testimony of priests and bishops should be given priority over the people who accuse them of crimes. Patronage determines who is employed and advanced in the church. All matters that impinge on reputation, particularly those that are sexual in nature, should be concealed under the cloak of charitable discretion.

Because priests and bishops oversee virtually all of the Catholic Church's subsidiary organizations, including those sponsored and run by religious sisters, their informal rules for responding to scandal have seeped into Catholic organizations. Our participants reported this differential discipline and treatment of priests in Catholic schools, universities, national youth organizations, dioceses, and parishes. They reported that people in Catholic schools, universities, and other organizations just disappear without any clear reason. The reasons for disappearing are varied, but the secrecy prevents shared analysis and solutions to problematic behavior, whether the person was dismissed for sexual harassment, misuse of funds, or incompetence. The emphasis on privacy and reputation is preventing us from learning how to be better. However, there is an alternative to the apologetics of perfection that is grounded in the apostolic tradition.

THE APOLOGETICS OF HUMILITY

The apologetics of humility are ultimately grounded in the revelation conveyed to us through the incarnation. Early Christians had to explain why the Messiah was conceived out of wedlock, born in a manger, raised as a carpenter, and died on the cross. When they experienced persecution and moral failures, they began to associate these problems with the ongoing passion of the body of Christ. If salvation comes through a humble and wounded Messiah, then a humble and wounded church can still be a viable means for salvation. The apologetics of humility emerged from reflecting on the humility of Jesus Christ.[25]

Augustine was instrumental in popularizing and justifying the apologetics of humility. He was responding to the Donatists, who wanted to establish a pure church. Augustine argued that the church, as we experience it in history, is always a mixed reality. Though the church is the body of Christ, he said that people must distinguish between the body and the head. The head, Jesus Christ, is without sin; but the body, which is made up of us, sins and falls short in many ways.[26]

Gregory the Great applied Augustine's ideas to his own exegetical endeavors, but his application of these ideas to the problems of pastoral care gave the apologetics of humility practical relevance. Gregory faced a multitude of problems with the clergy that ranged from greed to sexual abuse to forced conversions and even murder.[27] Throughout his career, Gregory had to respond to the question of why there are so many evil people, including priests and bishops, in the church. His answer was that God uses the people we despise in order to save us.[28] The malicious or evil members of the church serve an important soteriological function by helping the faithful to grow in holiness.

The heretics, according to Gregory, are those who fail to recognize the validity of flawed church and clergy. Instead of accepting the wounded church, the heretics imagine a perfect church and a pure priesthood. By trying to defend the perfection of God's church, he concluded, they came to offend God.[29] Ultimately, Gregory argued that their failure to exhibit patience in the face of ecclesial shortcomings revealed their lack of love.

Citing Galatians 6:2, Gregory explained that it is necessary to bear one another's sins in order to fulfill the law of Christ; however, he taught that people who committed scandalous acts were not fit for public office. Those who follow the law of Christ, he continued, are those who do not fall away when they are struck by scandal.[30] He argued that Christians are purified by accepting these burdens. The heretics, on the other hand, suffer from a triumphalist form of ecclesiology. As a result, the heretics fail to recognize the wounded church and recapitulate the sin of those who rejected Christ's divinity because of the scandal of the cross.[31]

The apologetics of humility were adopted by many medieval doctors of the church including Peter Damian, Bernard of Clairvaux, and Bonaventure. More recently, the apologetics of humility were promoted by *Lumen Gentium*:

> "Though he was in the 'form of God,' Christ Jesus emptied himself, taking the form of a servant" (Philemon 2:6–7); and for our sake "though he was rich he became poor" (2 Corinthians 8:9). So also the church, though it needs human resources to carry out its mission, is not set up to seek earthly glory, but to spread humility and self-denial also through its own example....While Christ "holy, blameless, unstained" (Hebrews 7:26) knew no sin, and came only to expiate the sins of the people, the church, containing sinners in its own bosom, is at one and the same time holy and always in need of purification and it always pursues unceasingly penance and renewal.[32]

The Council explained that the pilgrim church draws its strength to overcome its internal failures from the power of the risen Lord rather than those who commend themselves as holy (see 2 Cor 10:17–18).

In Christian spirituality, humility is a virtue that requires self-knowledge. Virtues are sources of power. Humility, which requires self-knowledge, frees people from pretension and excessive concern for their reputation. Pretension and vanity are parasitic in that they require an investment of time and energy to appear to be something we are not. Humble people also recognize the vanity and pretensions of others, emboldening them to speak truth to the pretensions of power—including the pretensions of priests, bishops, cardinals, and popes.

Organizations can be humble, at least by analogy. Organizational humility also requires self-knowledge. Organizations that create the processes and structures to learn their strengths and weaknesses are more likely to avoid the lure of wishful thinking. Humble organizations would recognize how establishing mimics rob functional capacity in the future. By sharing what they learn from their assessments broadly, they manage the expectations of their members and incentivize them to tackle problems. In this way, they avoid undercutting their credibility through premature load bearing.

What would it mean for the Catholic Church to spread humility by its own example as called for by Vatican II? A humble church would be relieved of the effort to project an image of perfection. Humility is a necessary condition for sustainable reforms, but it is not sufficient. Admitting imperfection is not equivalent to having an accurate assessment of organizational deficiencies or an understanding of what should be done. In addition to being humble, the Catholic Church needs to engage in an honest and rigorous assessment of how it is serving the mission. By dropping the pretension of perfection and creating a culture of continual assessment and improvement, the Catholic Church would be able not only to see but also to embark on the path to being better.

Recovering a humble church will require humility on the part of those of us who wish to see sustainable reform. We should expect opposition to the idea that the Catholic Church must move beyond merely consulting with the laity to establishing forms of shared governance. We must not let this opposition deter us from our commitment to foster cooperation and collaboration between the laity and clergy. Becoming a church that manifests equality, mutuality, and dynamism of the Trinity will require the expertise and gifts of the entire community. The path will be difficult. Deconstructing clericalism means picking up the cross and following Christ's example of self-denial, but on the other side, we have the promise of a communal resurrection and a new Pentecost.

NOTES

PREFACE

1. Albert O. Hirschman, *Exit, Voice, and Loyalty: Responses to Declines in Firms, Organizations, and States* (Harvard University Press, 1972).

2. C. Colt Anderson, *A Call to Piety: Bonaventure's Collations on the Six Days* (Franciscan Press, 2002).

3. Bonaventure, *Conferences on the Six Days of Creation*, 20.14-20. The newest English translation is *Conferences on the Six Days*, trans. and ed. Jay M. Hammond (Franciscan Institute Publications, 2018). The critical edition is in *S. Bonaventurae opera theologica selecta*, vol. 5 (Collegio S. Bonaventura, 1882).

4. C. Colt Anderson, "Bonaventure and the Sin of the Church," *Theological Studies* 63 (2002): 683.

5. Peter Damian, Letter 87.8. The English translation I am using is from the series *Peter Damian: Letters*, vols. 1–7, trans. Owen J. Blum and Irven M. Resnick (The Catholic University of America Press, 1989–2005). The numbering of the letters in the translation follows the critical edition *Die Briefe des Petrus Damiani*, ed. Kurt Reindel, *Monumenta Germaniae Historica: Die Briefe der deutschen Kaiserzeit*, vols. 1–4 (1983).

6. Peter Damian, Letter 61.4.

7. J. D. Long García, "Is There a Sexual Abuse Reckoning Ahead for Latino U.S. Catholics?," *America*, September 3, 2018, 13; J. D. Long García, "We Cannot Let the Sexual Abuse Crisis Lead Us into Homophobia," *America*, September 7, 2018, https://www.americamagazine.org/

faith/2018/09/07/we-cannot-let-sexual-abuse-crisis-lead-us-homo phobia.

8. Long García, "Reckoning," 13.

9. J. D. Long García, "At Fifth National Encuentro, Young Latino Catholics Are Ready to Lead," *America*, October 15, 2018, 16.

10. J. D. Long García, "Lessons Long Overdue: The Wrong People Are in Charge of Protecting Our Children from Sexual Abuse," *America*, January 1, 2021, 50–51.

11. Long García, "Lessons Long Overdue," 51.

12. Elie Wiesel, "Acceptance Speech," accessed at https://www.nobelprize.org/prizes/peace/1986/wiesel/acceptance-speech/#:~:text=And%20that%20is%20why%20I,the%20tormentor%2C%20never%20the%20tormented.

13. These patterns and incentives are what Douglass North calls "institutions" or the "rules of the game."

14. All of our citations of scripture are drawn from the New Revised Standard Version; however, many of our sources cite other editions that we have left as is in the text.

CHAPTER 1—CHANGING THE RULES OF THE GAME

1. Douglass C. North, "The Role of Institutions in Economic Development," United Nations Economic Commission for Europe Discussion Papers Series (Geneva: United Nations, 2003), 4, accessed September 9, 2019, https://www.unece.org/fileadmin/DAM/oes/disc_papers/ECE_DP_2003-2.pdf. Sections of this chapter were originally published in an article for *Horizons*. See C. Colt Anderson, "The Church as a Fragile State: A New Institutional Model for Understanding the Persistence of the Sexual Abuse Crisis," *Horizons* (December 2024): 233–69.

2. Douglass C. North, *Institutions, Institutional Change and Economic Performance* (Cambridge University Press, 1990), 3.

3. Adrian Leftwich and Kunal Sen, "Beyond Institutions: Institutions and Organizations in the Politics and Economics of Growth and Poverty Reduction—a Thematic Synthesis of Research Evidence" (DFID-Funded Research Programme Consortium on Improving Institutions for Pro-Poor Growth, University of Manchester, 2010), 7–66 at 16–17, https://assets.publishing.service.gov.uk/media/

57a08b00e5274a31e00008e8/8933_Beyond-Institutions-final.pdf. See also K. Collins, "Clans, Pacts and Politics in Central Asia," *Journal of Democracy* 13, no. 3 (2002): 137–52, http://muse.jhu.edu/journals/journal_of_democracy/v013/13.3collins.pdf.

4. Secretariat of Child and Youth Protection, *2021 Annual Report: Findings and Recommendations*, 14–15, accessed on February 11, 2023, https://www.usccb.org/resources/2021%20CYP%20Annual%20Report.PDF%20(1).pdf.

5. Pope Francis, *Christus Vivit* (Libreria Editrice Vaticana, 2018), 98, https://www.vatican.va/content/francesco/en/apost_exhortations/documents/papa-francesco_esortazione-ap_20190325_christus-vivit.html.

6. Congregation for the Clergy, "The Gift of Priestly Vocation," *L'Osservatore Romano* (December 8, 2016), 19, https://www.clerus.va/content/dam/clerus/documenti/ratio-2026/Ratio-EN-2017-01-03.pdf.

7. Leo XIII, *Depuis le jour* (Encyclical on the Education of the Clergy, September 8, 1899), 26, accessed January 11, 2023, https://www.vatican.va/content/leo-xiii/en/encyclicals/documents/hf_l-xiii_enc_08091899_depuis-le-jour.html. Leo XII wrote, "The Church historian will be all the better equipped to bring out her divine origin, superior as this is to all conceptions of a merely terrestrial and natural order, the more loyal he is in naught extenuating of the trials which the faults of her children, and at times even of her ministers, have brought upon the Spouse of Christ during the course of centuries. Studied in this way, the history of the Church constitutes by itself a magnificent and conclusive demonstration of the truth and divinity of Christianity."

8. The Australian Royal Commission into Institutional Responses to Child Sexual Abuse, *Final Report: Religious Institutions*, vol. 16:1 (Commonwealth of Australia, 2017), 43, accessed June 14, 2023, https://www.childabuseroyalcommission.gov.au/sites/default/files/final_report_-_volume_16_religious_institutions_book_1.pdf.

9. Australian Royal Commission into Institutional Responses to Child Sexual Abuse, *Final Report*, 41.

10. Australian Royal Commission into Institutional Responses to Child Sexual Abuse, *Final Report*, 43.

11. Avery Dulles, SJ, *Models of the Church*, expanded ed. (Image Books, 2002), 35. As we shall see, there is a historical connection between the model of the church as a perfect society and an effort to free the clergy from secular or lay oversight.

12. Dulles, *Models of the Church*, 29–30, 35.

13. Pseudo-Dionysius the Areopagite, *Ecclesiastical Hierarchy*, 5.1–6.3.

14. Thomas Aquinas, *Contra Impugnantes dei Cultum et Religionem* in *Sancti Thomae de Aquino Opera Omnia*, vol. 41 (Santa Sabina, 1969–1970), A55–57. Yves Congar pointed out that Robert Bellarmine divides his *Controversia de Ecclesia Militante* into three books focusing on the hierarchy of clergy, laity, and religious. See Yves Congar, *Lay People in the Church*, 2nd. ed. (Newman Press, 1965), 48–49.

15. Bonaventure, *Collations on the Six Days of Creation*, 22.17. The best English translation is *Conferences on the Six Days*, trans. and ed. Jay M. Hammond (Franciscan Institute Publications, 2018).

16. Dogmatic Constitution on the Church (*Lumen Gentium*), 30 in *Decrees of the Ecumenical Councils*, ed. Norman P. Tanner, 2 vols. (Georgetown University Press, 1990), 2:854 All citations of the Second Vatican are from this volume and will be identified by their Latin titles followed by the section number.

17. Pope Francis, *Vos Estis Lux Mundi* (May 7, 2019), prologue, http://w2.vatican.va/content/francesco/en/motu_proprio/documents/papa-francesco-motu-proprio-20190507_vos-estis-lux-mundi.html, accessed August 24, 2019.

18. Robert M. Cover, "The Supreme Court, 1982 Term—Foreword: Nomos and Narrative" (1983), accessed September 7, 2019, https://digitalcommons.law.yale.edu/fss_papers/2705/.

19. *Lumen Gentium* 1. Hereinafter cited in the text as *LG*.

20. The primary evangelists in the early church were religious men and women. Actually, women played a much more prominent role in evangelization than most Catholics realize as is evident in the case of St. Leoba. See Marie Anne Mayeski, "New Voices in the Tradition: Medieval Hagiography Revisited," *Theological Studies* 62 (2002): 690–710.

21. Fordham IRB Protocol 1704: "Identifying and Reforming Institutions in Jesuit Schools and Universities That Foster Sexual Abuse and Its Concealment" (approved November 16, 2020). Though the IRB Protocol title only mentions Jesuit schools and universities, the study included other Catholic schools and universities as well as Catholic organizations that work with vulnerable people, particularly those that work with children, youth, and young adults. We sent out over two hundred invitations to participate, and thirty-nine people accepted those invitations.

22. The seminal article on institutional isomorphism is Paul J. DiMaggio and Walter W. Powell, "The Iron Cage Revisited: Institutional Isomorphism and Collective Rationality in Organizational Fields," *American Sociological Review* 48 (1983): 147–60.

23. Secretariat of Child and Youth Protection, *2021 Annual Report: Findings and Recommendations*, 15–16.

24. Reese Dunklin et al., "Catholic Boards Hailed as a Fix for Sex Abuse Often Fail," *Associated Press*, November 20, 2019, https://apnews.com/article/wa-state-wire-mi-state-wire-id-state-wire-ct-state-wire-wv-state-wire-66ffb032675b4e599eb77c0875718dd4.

25. Dunklin et al., "Catholic Boards." The process that religious orders follow is similar; see Praesidium, *Accreditation Standards for Catholic Men's Religious Institutes 2020*, https://www.jesuits.org/wp-content/uploads/2021/04/Accreditation-Standards-for-Religious-Institutes_2020.pdf.

26. United States Conference of Catholic Bishops (USCCB), *Program for Priestly Formation* (2022), 142.

27. USCCB, *Program for Priestly Formation*, 142.

28. USCCB, *Program for Priestly Formation*, 43.

29. Australian Royal Commission into Institutional Responses to Child Sexual Abuse, *Identifying and Disclosing Child Sexual Abuse*, 4:146.

30. Australian Royal Commission into Institutional Responses to Child Sexual Abuse, *Identifying and Disclosing Child Sexual Abuse*, 146.

31. Neil Ormerod, "A Voice Cries in the Wilderness: The Place of the Social Sciences in Ecclesiology," in *A Realist's Church: Essays in Honor of Joseph A. Komonchak*, ed. Christopher D. Denny et al. (Orbis Books, 2015). Ormerod was a student of Komonchak, who has been arguably the leading ecclesiologist in the U.S. for the last thirty years. They follow the methods laid out by the Jesuit theologian Bernard Lonergan. While we respect Lonergan's work, we are not using his methods.

32. See, for example, William T. Ditewig, *Courageous Humility: Reflections on the Church, Diakonia, and Deacons* (Paulist Press, 2022).

CHAPTER 2—IDENTIFYING THE TRAP

1. Pope Francis, "Address to the Leadership of the Episcopal Conferences of Latin America During the General Coordination Meeting" (Sunday, July 28, 2013), sec. 4.

2. Douglass C. North, *Institutions, Institutional Change and Economic Performance* (Cambridge University Press, 1990), 23, 26, 57.

3. North, *Institutions*, 99.

4. North, *Institutions*, 99.

5. *Decrees of the Ecumenical Councils*, ed. Norman P. Tanner, 2 vols. (Sheed and Ward, 1990), 2:663. This is the first decree from session 4.

6. John Paul II, *Ordinatio Sacerdotalis*, 4, accessed June 15, 2023, https://www.vatican.va/content/john-paul-ii/en/apost_letters/1994/documents/hf_jp-ii_apl_19940522_ordinatio-sacerdotalis.html.

7. John Henry Newman, *On Consulting the Faithful in Matters of Doctrine* (Sheed and Ward, 1961), 63–75.

8. Newman, *On Consulting the Faithful*, 75.

9. Joint Statement of the Dicasteries for Culture and Education and for Promoting Integral Human Development on the "Doctrine of Discovery," (March 30, 2023), §6, accessed June 15, 2023, https://press.vatican.va/content/salastampa/en/bollettino/pubblico/2023/03/30/230330b.html.

10. This paragraph and the following paragraphs summarize the discussion of the debate over tradition in George Tavard, *Holy Writ or Holy Church: The Crisis of the Protestant Reformation* (New Harper, 1959), 195–209.

11. Tavard, *Holy Writ or Holy Church*, 204.

12. Geoffrey M. Hodgson, "What Are Institutions?" *Journal of Economic Issues* 40 (2006): 10.

13. Douglass North, "The Role of Institutions in Economic Development," Discussion Paper Series (October 2003) United Nations Economic Commission for Europe, 1.

14. *Lumen Gentium* 1 in *Decrees of the Ecumenical Councils*, 2:849.

15. *Lumen Gentium* 1. See also Adrian Leftwich and Kunal Sen, "Beyond Institutions: Institutions and Organizations in the Politics and Economics of Growth and Poverty Reduction—a Thematic Synthesis of Research Evidence" (DFID-Funded Research Programme Consortium on Improving Institutions for Pro-Poor Growth, University of Manchester, 2010), 46–50.

16. Eileen Munro and Sheila Fish, *Hear No Evil, See No Evil: Understanding Failure to Identify and Report Child Sexual Abuse in Institutional Contexts* (Royal Commission into Institutional Responses to Child Sexual Abuse, 2015), 13.

17. Munro and Fish, *Hear No Evil*, 19. The study cites D. Kahneman et al., *Judgement Under Uncertainty: Heuristics and Biases* (Cambridge University Press, 1982), 464.

18. Munro and Fish, *Hear No Evil*, 21–22.

19. Munro and Fish, *Hear No Evil*, 19–21.

20. Secretariat of State of the Holy See, Report on the Holy See's Institutional Knowledge and Decision-Making Related to Former Cardinal Theodore Edgar McCarrick (Vatican City, 2020), 7, accessed on February 11, 2023, https://www.vatican.va/resources/resources_rapporto-card-mccarrick_20201110_en.pdf. Hereafter cited as *The Cardinal McCarrick Report*.

21. *The Cardinal McCarrick Report*, 9.

22. *Lumen Gentium* 25, *Decrees of the Ecumenical Councils*, 2:869, 872; *Catechism of the Catholic Church*, 2nd ed. (Libreria Editrice Vaticana, 2000), 888, 896, 757, 796, https://www.vatican.va/archive/ENG0015/_INDEX.HTM.

23. John Cardinal O'Conner, "The Necessity for the Ongoing Formation for the Priest," *The Holy See*. Published June 18, 1996, and accessed May 9, 2015. http://www.vatican.va/roman_curia/congregations/cclergy/documents/rc_con_cclergy_doc_18061996_intr_en.html.

24. Robert N. Swanson, "Apostolic Successors: Priests and Priesthood, Bishops, and Episcopacy in Medieval Western Europe," in *Priesthood and Holy Orders in the Middle Ages*, ed. Greg Peters and C. Colt Anderson (Brill, 2016), 10–11, 31.

25. The Code of Canon Law, 292, accessed June 15, 2023, https://www.vatican.va/archive/cod-iuris-canonici/eng/documents/cic_lib2-cann208-329_en.html#:~:text=290%20Once%20validly%20received%2C%20sacred%20ordination%20never%20becomes%20invalid.

26. Richard R. Gaillardetz, *Ecclesiology for a Global Church: A People Called and Sent* (Orbis Press), 32. Chapter 1 of this book provides an excellent summary of the history of the early church.

27. Bernard of Clairvaux, *On Consideration*, 2.6.10. The translation I am using is *Five Books On Consideration: Advice to a Pope*, trans. John D. Anderson and Elizabeth T. Keenan (Cistercian Publications, 1976).

28. Bernard of Clairvaux, *On Consideration*, 1.6.7.

29. Bernard of Clairvaux, *On Consideration*, 3.1.1.

30. Peter Damian, Letter 65.26. The translation I use is from *Peter Damian: Letters*, vols. 1–7, trans. Owen J. Blum and Irven M. Resnick,

The Fathers of the Church: Medieval Continuation (The Catholic University of America Press, 1989–2005). For more detailed analysis see C. Colt Anderson, "When Magisterium Becomes Imperium: St. Peter Damian on the Accountability of Bishops for Scandal," *Theological Studies*, 65 (2004): 741–66.

31. Geoffrey M Hodgson, "What Are Institutions?," 13–16.

32. The following paragraphs were the source for C. Colt Anderson, "The Church as a Fragile State: A New Institutional Model for Understanding the Persistence of the Sexual Abuse Crisis," *Horizons* (December 2024): 1–37.

33. "The Church as a Fragile State," 6–7. The seminal article on institutional isomorphism is Paul J. DiMaggio and Walter W. Powell, "The Iron Cage Revisited: Institutional Isomorphism and Collective Rationality in Organizational Fields," *American Sociological Review* 48 (1983): 147–60.

34. Lant Pritchett and Frauke de Weijer, "Fragile States: Stuck in a Capability Trap?," World Development Report 2011 Background Paper (World Bank, 2010), 27.

35. Pritchett and de Weijer, "Fragile States," 28.

36. See Cardinal Joseph Ratzinger, Declaration *Dominus Iesus* on the Unicity and Salvific Universality of Jesus Christ and the Church (Offices of the Congregation of the Faith), 20 and 21, accessed February 13, 2023, https://www.vatican.va/roman_curia/congregations/cfaith/documents/rc_con_cfaith_doc_20000806_dominus-iesus_en.html. See also *Lumen Gentium* 14, 860.

37. Pritchett and de Weijer, "Fragile States," 2.

38. Pritchett and de Weijer, "Fragile States," 6.

39. Pritchett and de Weijer, "Fragile States," 2.

40. Matt Andrews et al., "The Challenge of Building (Real) State Capability," Center for International Development at Harvard University Working Papers no. 306 (December 2015), 22.

41. Andrews et al., "The Challenge of Building (Real) State Capability," 240.

42. Andrews et al., "The Challenge of Building (Real) State Capability," 240.

43. Pritchett and de Weijer, "Fragile States," 2.

44. Lant Pritchett et al., "Capability Traps? The Mechanisms of Persistent Implementation Failure," *Working Paper* 234 (Center for Global Development, 2010), 37.

45. Pritchett and de Weijer, "Fragile States," 28.

46. Pritchett and de Weijer, "Fragile States," 28.

47. Tom Reese, SJ, "U.S. Catholic Bishops Adopt Process for Reviewing Misconduct of Bishops," *National Catholic Reporter*, June 17, 2019, accessed August 24, 2019, https://www.ncronline.org/news/accountability/signs-times/us-catholic-bishops-adopt-process-reviewing-misconduct-bishops; John L. Allen, "Thoughts on Populism, Liability, and Unfinished Business on Abuse Norms," *Crux*, May 12, 2019, accessed August 24, 2019, https://cruxnow.com/news-analysis/2019/05/thoughts-of-populism-liability-and-unfinished-business-on-abuse-norms; J. D. Flynn, "Analysis: Is Pope Francis' New Abuse Plan the Answer Catholics Are Looking For?," *Catholic News Agency*, May 9, 2019, accessed August 24, 2019, https://www.catholicnewsagency.com/news/analysis-is-pope-francis-new-abuse-plan-the-answer-catholics-are-looking-for-32480.

CHAPTER 3—A HISTORY OF CLERICALISM

1. This is Anderson's translation from the Latin Vulgate (*Spiritualis autem judicat omnia: et ipse a nemine judicatur*), which is closer to the various editions employed in the early and medieval church in the West. It was not until the Council of Trent that the Vulgate edition was declared the standard translation. Anderson could have declined to include *ipse* as "himself" to render the passage more gender neutral, but it would be a violation of how this passage was used and understood. We should use gender-inclusive language in contemporary translations, but history requires us to pay attention to how these texts have functioned over time.

2. The translation is from John Meyendorff, *Imperial Unity and Christian Divisions* (St. Vladimir's Seminary Press, 1989), 161. Gelasius's letter is Epistle 9 in *Patrologiae latinae cursus completus*, vol. 59, edited by J. P. Migne (Paris, 1844–1866).

3. For a brief overview, see John Meyendorff, *Imperial Unity and Christian Divisions*, 162–64.

4. *Code of Canon Law*, Canon 1404, accessed on May 23, 2023, https://www.vatican.va/archive/cod-iuris-canonici/eng/documents/cic_lib7-cann1400-1500_en.html.

5. Eric Knibbs, "Ebo of Reims, Pseudo-Isidore, and the Date of the False Decretals," *Speculum* 92, no. 1 (January 2017): 181.

6. Knibbs, "Ebo of Reims," 155–57.

7. Anderson has written about the ways that exhortatory models become definitions of priesthood in "Reforming Priests in the High Middle Ages: The Diverse Rhetorics of Ordination and Office 1123–1418," in *Priesthood and Holy Orders in the Middle Ages*, ed. Greg Peterson and C. Colt Anderson (Brill, 2015), 281–306.

8. John W. O'Malley, SJ, "The Hermeneutic of Reform: A Historical Analysis," *Theological Studies* 73 (2012): 524. O'Malley's discussion of institutional reform is consistent with North's use of the term. For a recent study on Gregory VII see Ken A. Grant, "Pope Gregory VII's Idea of Reform," in *Reassessing Reform: A Historical Investigation into Church Renewal*, ed. Christopher M. Bellitto and David Zachariah Flanagin (The Catholic University of America Press, 2012), 61–83.

9. Colin Morris, *The Papal Monarchy: The Western Church from 1050–1250* (Clarendon Press, 1989), 28–30.

10. One difficulty was the general attitude in the tenth and early part of the eleventh centuries was that it was impossible to follow all the details of canon law. See Heinrich Fichtenau, *Living in the Tenth Century: Mentalities and Social Orders*, trans. Patrick J. Geary (The University of Chicago Press, 1991), 118.

11. Morris, *The Papal Monarchy*, 60–62.

12. Gregory VII, *The Register of Pope Gregory VII 1073–1085*, trans. H. E. J. Cowdrey (Oxford University Press, 2002), 392. This is letter 8.21 in the register. The Latin edition is in *Das Register Gregors VII*, ed. Erich Caspar, in *Monumenta Germaniae Historica* (Weidmannsche Buchhandlung, 1920–23).

13. Gregory VII, *The Register of Pope Gregory VII*, 392.

14. Owen J. Blum, *St. Peter Damian: His Teaching on the Spiritual Life* (The Catholic University of America Press, 1947), 19–22. Anderson has written about Peter Damian's reform efforts and theology in "When Magisterium Becomes Imperium: St. Peter Damian on the Accountability of the Bishops," *Theological Studies* 65 (2004): 741–66.

15. Peter Damian, Letter 40.5. The English translation is from *Peter Damian: Letters*, trans. Owen J. Blum and Irven M. Resnick, The Fathers of the Church: Medieval Continuation, vol. 2 (The Catholic University of America Press, 1989–2005).

16. Gregory VII, *The Register of Pope Gregory VII*, 390.

17. The translation is from Peter J. Leithart, "The Gospel, Gregory VII, and Modern Theology," *Modern Theology* 19 (January 2003): 11. Leithart argued that the term *lay* took on a negative connotation

after Gregory VII. There is a relatively new critical edition *Die Chroniken Bertholds von Reichenau Und Bernolds von Konstanz 1054–1100*, ed. I. S. Robinson (Hahnsche Buchhandlung, 2003).

18. Hugh of St. Victor, *De sacramentis Christianae fidei* II.2.4; Gratian, *Decretum* C. 12 q.1 c. 7 and D. 96 c. 9–10.

19. Innocent III, "On the Consecration of the Supreme Pontiff," in *Between God and Man: Six Sermons on the Priestly Office*, trans. Corinne J. Vause and Frank C. Gardiner (The Catholic University of America Press, 2004), 23. This is sermon 2 in *Patrologiae cursus completes…series Latina*, ed. J.-P. Migne (Paris, 1844–1864), vol. 217.

20. *Decrees of the Ecumenical Councils*, ed. Norman P. Tanner, vol. 1 (Sheed and Ward, 1990), 236.

21. Innocent III, "On the Consecration of the Supreme Pontiff," trans. Corinne J. Vause and Frank C. Gardiner in *Between God and Man* (The Catholic University of America Press, 2004), 23.

22. Pope Innocent III, *In Council of Priests*, 10.

23. Pope Innocent III, *In Council of Priests*, 13–14.

24. Mary Douglas, *Purity and Danger: An Analysis of Concepts of Pollution and Taboo* (Routledge, 1977), 132–33.

25. Gratian, *Decretum*, D. 5 c. 4–6.

26. Gratian, *Decretum*, D.5 c. 6.

27. See Morris, *Papal Monarchy*, 100: "There is little in the whole literature of the papal reform movement about the need to make the clergy personally more devout, to build up their character, or to provide better instruction or pastoral care for the laity. Indeed, there is only a limited amount of discussion designed to define the priestly office in its inner character. These things do indeed become important in the thirteenth century, but in the age of Leo IX and Gregory VII we are still in a primitive society, in which it is more accurate to think in terms of cultic reform."

28. Morris, *Papal Monarchy*, 100.

29. Fourth Lateran Council, in *Decrees of the Ecumenical Councils*, ed. Norman P. Tanner, vol. 1 (Washington, DC: Sheed and Ward, 1990), 237–38.

30. Fourth Lateran Council, *Decrees*, 237–38.

31. Fourth Lateran Council, *Decrees*, 255.

32. *Giles of Rome's On Ecclesiastical Power: A Medieval Theory of World Government*, ed. and trans. R. W. Dyson (Columbia University Press, 2004), 26–27. The Latin edition is *De ecclesiastica potestate*, ed. Richard Scholz (H. Böhlaus Nachfolger, 1929).

33. *Giles of Rome's On Ecclesiastical Power*, 11.

34. Brian Tierney, *The Crisis of Church and State 1050–1300* (Prentice-Hall, 1964; repr., University of Toronto Press, 1988), 188.

35. Christopher M. Bellitto, "The Reform Context of the Great Western Schism," in *A Companion to the Great Western Schism (1378–1417)*, ed. Joel Rollo-Koster and Thomas Izbicki (Brill, 2009), 303. This article was the original impetus for studying institutions as understood in disciplines such a political science and economics.

36. Gerhart B. Ladner, *The Idea of Reform: Its Impact on Christian Thought and Action in the Age of the Fathers* (Harvard University Press, 1959).

37. For examples of this understanding of reform see Louis B. Pascoe, SJ, *Church and Reform: Bishops, Theologians, and Canon Lawyers in the Thought of Pierre D'Ailly, 1351–1420* (Brill 2005); Phillip H. Stump, *The Reforms of the Council of Constance (1414–1418)* (Brill, 1994).

38. For a concise history see C. Colt Anderson, "Reforming Priests and the Diverse Rhetorics of Ordination and Office from 1123–1418," in *Priesthood and Holy Orders in the Middle Ages*, ed. Greg Peterson and C. Colt Anderson (Brill, 2015), 281–306.

39. John Olin, *Catholic Reform: From Cardinal Ximenes to the Council of Trent* (Fordham University Press, 1990), 36. See also John C. Olin, *The Catholic Reformation: Savonarola to Ignatius Loyola* (Fordham University Press, 1992), xvi–xix.

40. Jean Gerson, *De auferibilitate sponsi ab Ecclesia*, in *Oeuvres complètes*, vol. 3 (1962), 300.

41. For a detailed account of Gerson's argument see Louis Pascoe, *Jean Gerson: Principles of Church Reform* (Brill, 1973), 43–48. Jean Gerson, *De auferibilitate sponsi ab Ecclesia*, 297.

42. Gerson, *De auferibilitate sponsi ab Ecclesia*, 301; Gerson, *De unitate Ecclesia*, in *Oeuvres complètes*, vol. 6 (1965), 143.

43. Gerson, *De unitate Ecclesia*, 143.

44. Council of Constance, in *Decrees of the Ecumenical Councils*, 1:408.

45. Council of Constance, in *Decrees of the Ecumenical Councils*, 1:447–50.

46. Council of Constance, in *Decrees of the Ecumenical Councils*, 1:439.

47. Bellitto, "The Reform Context of the Great Schism," 330.

48. Steven Ozment, *The Age of Reform 1250–1550* (Yale University Press, 190), 173.

49. Bernhard Schimmelpfennig, *The Papacy*, trans. James Sievert (Columbia University Press, 1992), 234.

50. Ozment, *The Age of Reform*, 188.

51. Gregory XVI, *Mirari Vos* 10. The Latin text can be found in *Acta Gregorii Papae XVI*, ed. A. M. Bernasconius, vol. 1 (Rome, 1901), 169–74.

52. Pius IX, *Pii IX Pontificis Acta*, Pars Prima, vol. 3 (no date), 701–17; Pius X, *Sacrorum Antistitum*, http://www.vatican.va/content/pius-x/la/motu_proprio/documents/hf_p-x_motu-proprio_19100901_sacrorum-antistitum.html.

53. Bellitto, "Reform Context of the Great Western Schism," 304. Bellitto provides a historiographical review of the literature on ecclesial reform in the late Middle Ages in this article.

54. *Catechism of the Catholic Church*, 2nd ed. (Libreria Editrice Vaticana, 2000), 878.

55. *Catechism of the Catholic Church* 888. The source is *Lumen Gentium* 25. We cite the catechism to indicate how widely diffused these ideas are. The catechism shapes what Catholics are taught to think about the church and holy orders from an early age.

56. *Catechism of the Catholic Church* 757 and 796. The source is *Lumen Gentium* 6.

57. *Catechism of the Catholic Church* 825. See *Lumen Gentium* 48.

58. Donald W. Wuerl, "Reflections on Governance and Accountability in the Church," in *Governance, Accountability, and the Future of the Catholic Church*, ed. Francis Oakley and Bruce Russett (Continuum, 2004), 18. See also Richard Gaillardetz, *By What Authority? Foundations for Understanding Authority in the Church*, rev. ed. (Liturgical Press, 2018), 22.

59. *Lumen Gentium* 8. In a similar vein, Henri De Lubac warned against deifying the church's visibility and rejected what he called a monophysite ecclesiology in *Catholicism: Christ and the Common Destiny of Man*, trans. Lancelot C. Sheppard and Sister Elizabeth Englund, OCD (Ignatius, 1988), 74–75.

60. The quotation is from John F. Wirenius, "Command and Coercion: Clerical Immunity, Scandal, and the Sexual Abuse Crisis in the Roman Catholic Church," *Journal of Law and Religion* vol. 27 (January 2011): 466. The following section on canon law relies on Wirenius's article and its translations.

61. Wirenius, "Command and Coercion," 466.

62. Wirenius, "Command and Coercion," 466–67.

63. Wirenius, "Command and Coercion," 468.

64. Wirenius, "Command and Coercion," 468–69.

65. Wirenius, "Command and Coercion," 470.

66. Wirenius, "Command and Coercion," 472–73.

67. Wirenius, "Command and Coercion," 473–74.

68. Kieran Tapsell, "A Systemic Factor in Child Sexual Abuse in the Catholic," Submission to the Royal Commission into Institutional Responses to Child Sexual Abuse (August 10, 2015), 82, accessed https://www.childabuseroyalcommission.gov.au/sites/default/files/SUBM.2398.001.0001.pdf. Cited as "Submission."

69. Wirenius, "Command and Coercion" 470–71; Tapsell, "Submission," 82–83.

70. Tapsell, "Submission," 81. He cited *Crimen Sollicitationis* 63. The text can be found in English and other languages on the Vatican website: https://www.vatican.va/resources/resources_crimen-sollicitationis-1962_en.html.

71. The Australian Royal Commission into Institutional Responses to Child Sexual Abuse, *Final Report: Religious Institutions*, vol. 16.1 (Commonwealth of Australia, 2017), 711–14.

72. Australian Royal Commission, *Final Report: Religious Institutions*, 84.

73. Thomas P. Doyle, "Book Offers Insight into Canon Law's Role in Sexual Abuse Crisis," *National Catholic Reporter*, April 22, 2015, accessed May 22, 2023: https://www.ncronline.org/books/2022/06/book-offers-insight-canon-laws-role-sexual-abuse-crisis.

74. Tapsell, "Submission," 94. See Can. 1321 §1: "No one is punished unless the external violation of a law or precept, committed by the person, is gravely imputable by reason of malice or negligence." See also Can. 1322: "Those who habitually lack the use of reason are considered to be incapable of a delict, even if they violated a law or precept while seemingly sane."

75. Tapsell, "Submission," 94. See Canons 1362 and 1395.

76. Tapsell, "Submission," 95.

77. Tapsell, "Submission," 114–15.

78. Pope Francis, *Vos Estis*, accessed May 5, 2022, https://www.vatican.va/content/francesco/en/motu_proprio/documents/papa-francesco-motu-proprio-20190507_vos-estis-lux-mundi.html.

79. Pope Francis, *Vos Estis*.

80. Joshua J. McElwee, "Francis Says He May Reconsider Convicted Cardinal's Resignation After Appeal," *National Catholic Reporter*, March 31, 2019.

CHAPTER 4—HOW CLERICALISM FOSTERS ABUSE IN THE CHURCH

1. See Donald Palmer, "Research Report: The Role of Organisational Culture in Child Sexual Abuse in Institutional Contexts" (Royal Commission into Institutional Responses to Child Sexual Abuse, 2016), accessed June 22, 2023. https://www.childabuseroyalcommission.gov.au/sites/default/files/file-list/Research%20Report%20-%20The%20role%20of%20organisational%20culture%20in%20child%20sexual%20abuse%20in%20institutional%20contexts%20-%20Causes.pdf.

2. Royal Commission into Institutional Responses to Child Sexual Abuse, *Final Report*, vol. 16, *Religious Institutes*, book 1 (Commonwealth of Australia, 2017), 16. This will be cited as Royal Commission *Final Report* with the volume number and title in the first reference and just the volume number in subsequent references.

3. Australian Bureau of Statistics (July 4, 2022), Religious Affiliation in Australia, ABS Website, accessed October 14, 2023, https://www.abs.gov.au/articles/religious-affiliation-Australia.

4. Faisal Rashid and Ian Barron, "Why the Focus of Clerical Child Sexual Abuse Has Largely Remained on the Catholic Church Amongst Other Non-Catholic Christian Denominations and Religions," *Journal of Child Sexual Abuse* 28 (2019): 576. This study provides a thorough review of the literature.

5. Rashid and Barron, "Why the Focus of Clerical Child Sexual Abuse," 576.

6. Royal Commission, *Final Report*, vol. 2: *Nature and Cause*, 99.

7. Royal Commission, *Final Report: Identifying and Disclosing Child Sexual Abuse*, vol. 4, 146.

8. Royal Commission, *Final Report*, vol. 4, 146.

9. Royal Commission, *Final Report*, vol. 4, 147.

10. Royal Commission, *Final Report*, vol. 2, 169.

11. Royal Commission, *Final Report*, vol. 2, 160.

12. Royal Commission, *Final Report*, vol. 2, 165.

13. Royal Commission, *Final Report*, vol. 2, 166.

14. Royal Commission, *Final Report*, vol. 16, 43.

15. Royal Commission, *Final Report*, vol. 16, 43.

16. Royal Commission, *Final Report*, vol. 16, 44.

17. Royal Commission, *Final Report*, vol. 16, 44.

18. Royal Commission, *Final Report*, vol. 16, 48.

19. Group interview with university and seminary administrators and faculty members in ministry programs.

20. Group interview with university and seminary administrators and faculty members in ministry programs.

21. Group interview with university and seminary administrators and faculty members in ministry programs; group interview with members of the Society of Jesus.

22. Group interview with university and seminary administrators and faculty members in ministry programs.

23. Group interview with national youth leaders.

24. Group interview with national youth leaders.

25. Group interview with members of the Society of Jesus.

26. Group interview with university and seminary administrators and faculty members in ministry programs.

27. Individual interview with member of the Society of Jesus.

28. Group interview with university and seminary administrators and faculty members; group interview with national youth leaders; individual interview with member of the Society of Jesus.

29. Group interview with university and seminary administrators and faculty members in ministry programs.

30. Individual interview with national Catholic lay leader.

31. Individual interview with lay diocesan leader.

32. Group interview with national youth leaders.

33. Group interview with university and seminary administrators and faculty members in ministry programs.

34. Individual interview with lay diocesan leader.

35. Group interview with retired members of the Society of Jesus.

36. Individual interview with national Catholic lay leader.

37. Individual interview with public safety professional.

38. Group interview with seminary faculty members.

39. Group interview with seminary faculty members.

40. Group interview with seminary faculty members.

41. Group interview with seminary faculty members.

42. Group interview with seminary faculty members.

43. Group interview with seminary faculty members.

44. Group interview with national youth leaders.

45. Group interview with members of the Society of Jesus.
46. Individual interview with member of the Society of Jesus.
47. Individual interview with member of the Society of Jesus.
48. Group interview with national Catholic lay leaders.
49. Group interview with national Catholic lay leaders.
50. Individual interview with Jesuit high school administrator.
51. Individual interview with Jesuit high school administrator.
52. Individual interview with lay diocesan leader.
53. Group interview with national youth leaders.
54. Individual interview with lay diocesan leader.
55. Group interview with national Catholic lay leaders.
56. Group interview with national Catholic lay leaders.
57. Group interview with national youth leaders.
58. Individual interview with national Catholic lay leader.
59. Group interview with university and seminary administrators and faculty members in ministry programs.
60. Group interview with university and seminary administrators and faculty members in ministry programs.
61. Individual interview with Jesuit high school administrator.
62. Group interview with national youth leaders.
63. Group interview with national Catholic lay leaders.
64. Group interview with national Catholic lay leaders.
65. Individual interview with lay diocesan leader.
66. Group interview with university and seminary administrators and faculty members in ministry programs.
67. Group interview with seminary faculty members.
68. Group interview with seminary faculty members.
69. Group interview with national Catholic lay leaders.
70. Individual interview with national Catholic lay leader.
71. Group interview with national Catholic lay leaders.
72. Jerry Filteau, "Cardinal Mahony Barred from Public Ministry in Los Angeles," *National Catholic Reporter*, Feb. 1, 2013. https://www.ncronline.org/news/accountability/cardinal-mahony-barred-public-ministry-los-angeles.
73. Filteau, "Cardinal Mahony Barred from Public Ministry in Los Angeles."
74. Group interview with graduates of doctoral program at Jesuit universities.
75. Group interview with university and seminary administrators and faculty members in ministry programs.

76. Group interview with university and seminary administrators and faculty members in ministry programs.

77. Group interview with graduates of doctoral program at Jesuit universities.

78. Group interview with Jesuit high school faculty.

79. Group interview with university and seminary administrators and faculty members in ministry programs.

80. Group interview with retired members of the Society of Jesus.

81. Individual interview with national Catholic lay leader.

82. Group interview with national Catholic lay leaders.

CHAPTER 5—THE EFFECTS OF CLERICALISM ON THE SOCIETY OF JESUS

1. Markus Friedrich, *The Jesuits: A History*, trans by John Noël Dillon (Princeton University Press: 2022), 17.

2. International Association of Jesuit Universities, https://iaju.org/. For more on the Jesuit influence on the Catholic Church in the United States, see Raymond A. Schroth, *The American Jesuits: A History* (NYU Press, 2009), and David J. Collins, *The Jesuits in the United States: A Concise History* (Georgetown University Press, 2023).

3. Group interview with members of the Society of Jesus.

4. Group interview with retired members of the Society of Jesus.

5. Group interview with members of the Society of Jesus.

6. Group interview with members of the Society of Jesus.

7. Group interview with university and seminary administrators and faculty members in ministry programs.

8. Group interview with university and seminary administrators and faculty members in ministry programs.

9. Group interview with Jesuit high school faculty.

10. Group interview with graduates of doctoral program at Jesuit universities.

11. Group interview with members of the Society of Jesus.

12. Vatican II, *Lumen Gentium* 43.

13. *The Constitutions of the Society of Jesus and Their Complementary Norms: A Complete and English Translation of the Official Latin Texts*, ed. John W. Padberg, SJ (The Institute of Jesuit Sources, 1996), 24. All the

references to the *Constitutions and Norms* are from this volume. For the sake of simplicity, we are referring to the page numbers in this volume rather than citing chapters and paragraph numbers. The *Constitutions* have two different numbering systems. When it comes to the *Complementary Norms*, we will identify the norm number in the main text but only the page numbers in the notes.

14. Vatican II, *Perfectae Caritatis* (Decree on the Sensitive Renewal of Religious Life), 2. Hereinafter referred to in the text as *PC*.

15. John W. O'Malley, SJ, *The First Jesuits* (Harvard University Press, 1993), 353.

16. Group interview with university and seminary administrators and faculty members in ministry programs.

17. O'Malley, *The First Jesuits*, 354.

18. *Constitutions and Complementary Norms*, 360–64 (736, 739, 740, 743, 755).

19. *Constitutions and Complementary Norms*, 364 (755). Hereinafter referred to in the text as *CCN*.

20. *Constitutions and Complementary Norms*, 93. Norm 33.

21. *Constitutions and Complementary Norms*, 96.

22. *Constitutions and Complementary Norms*, 101.

23. *Constitutions and Complementary Norms*, 102.

24. *Constitutions and Complementary Norms*, 354 (Norm 355 §2).

25. *Code of Canon Law*, canons 694–97.

26. *Constitutions and Complementary Norms*, 355 (Norm 357).

27. Royal Commission into Institutional Responses to Child Sexual Abuse, *Final Report*, vol. 16, *Religious Institutes* (Commonwealth of Australia, 2017), 45.

28. Australian Catholic Bishops Conference and Catholic Religious Australia, *Australian Conference of Bishops Conference and Catholic Religious of Australia's Response to the Royal Commission in Institutional Responses to Child Sexual Abuse* (August 2018), 12.

29. Gregory the Great justified speaking out publicly against wicked acts on the part of the ordained in *Pastoral Care*, 3.4. See C. Colt Anderson, *The Great Catholic Reformers: From Gregory the Great to Dorothy Day* (Paulist Press, 2007), 22–26.

30. For a discussion of this see Anderson, *The Great Catholic Reformers*, 50–51. See Peter Damian, Letter 54.12–16. All English translations of Peter Damian are from *Peter Damian: Letters*, vol. 1–7, trans. Owen J. Blum and Irven M. Resnick (The Catholic University of America Press, 1989–2005).

31. Peter Damian, Letter 61.4.

32. Group interview with members of the Society of Jesus.

33. Group interview with members of the Society of Jesus.

34. Group interview with members of the Society of Jesus.

35. Group interview with members of the Society of Jesus.

36. Pierre Favre, "Selected Letters and Instructions," trans. Martin E. Palmer, SJ, in *The Spiritual Writings of Pierre Favre* (The Institute of Jesuit Studies, 1996), 331.

37. Favre, "Selected Letters and Instructions," 331.

38. Favre, "Selected Letters and Instructions," 331.

39. Mark Chaves, "Rain Dances in the Dry Season: Overcoming the Religious Congruence Fallacy," *Journal for the Scientific Study of Religion* vol. 49, no. 1 (2010): 1.

40. Group interview with university and seminary administrators and faculty members in ministry programs.

41. Group interview with members of the Society of Jesus.

42. Group interview with retired members of the Society of Jesus.

43. Group interview with members of the Society of Jesus.

44. Group interview with members of the Society of Jesus.

45. Group interview with members of the Society of Jesus.

46. Individual interview with member of the Society of Jesus.

47. Group interview with members of the Society of Jesus.

48. Group interview with members of the Society of Jesus.

49. Group interview with members of the Society of Jesus.

50. Group interview with members of the Society of Jesus.

51. Group interview with members of the Society of Jesus.

52. Group interview with members of the Society of Jesus.

53. Group interview with members of the Society of Jesus.

54. Individual interview with members of the Society of Jesus.

55. Group interview with members of the Society of Jesus.

56. Group interview with members of the Society of Jesus.

57. Group interview with members of the Society of Jesus.

58. Group interview with members of the Society of Jesus.

59. Group interview with university and seminary administrators and faculty members in ministry programs.

60. Group interview with university and seminary administrators and faculty members in ministry programs.

61. Individual interview with Jesuit high school administrator.

62. Group interview with Jesuit high school faculty.

63. John O'Malley observed that Jesuit commentators on the *Constitutions* have argued that they are a translation of the *Exercises* into an institutional form. O'Malley conceded this interpretation as an exaggeration, but he affirmed that he believed it contains more than a grain of truth. O'Malley, *The First Jesuits*, 372–73.

64. Robert Hurley, "When Organizational Learning Disabilities Undermine Trust: An Exploration in the Context of the Child Sexual Abuse Crisis Within the Catholic Church," forthcoming.

65. Robert Hurley, "When Organizational Learning Disabilities Undermine Trust," draft, 9.

66. John Paul II, "Message for the 85th World Immigration Day," 2, §5, accessed March 14, 2024, https://w2.vatican.va/content/john-paul-ii/en/messages/migration/documents/hf_jp-ii_mes_22021999_world-migration-day-1999.html.

CHAPTER 6—HOW CLERICALISM LIMITS CAPACITY

1. See, for example, Michal J. Kramarek and Thomas P. Gaunt, "The Class of 2024: Survey of Ordinands to the Priesthood" (Center for Applied Research in the Apostolate, 2024).

2. See, for example, Marcus Pound and Gregory A. Ryan, "Attitudes of Catholics in England and Wales Towards Child Sex Abuse in the Catholic Church," from Centre from Catholic Studies at Durham University, April 2024, accessed Oct. 10, 2024, https://www.durham.ac.uk/media/durham-university/research-/research-centres/catholic-studies-centre-for-ccs/Boundary-Breaking-Quantitative-Report.pdf.

3. Group interview with national youth leaders.

4. Group interview with national youth leaders.

5. Group interview with university and seminary administrators and faculty members in ministry programs.

6. Group interview with national youth leaders.

7. Group interview with national youth leaders.

8. Individual interview with lay diocesan leader.

9. Individual interview with lay diocesan leader.

10. Group interview with national youth leaders.

11. Group interview with national youth leaders.

12. Pope Leo XIII, *Rerum Novarum* 44. Anderson has adjusted the translation in a few places to make the text more inclusive. Anderson is

using the translation provided on the Vatican website and its numbering system available from http://www.vatican.va/holy_father/leo_xiii/encyclicals/documents/hf_l-xiii_enc_15051891_rerum-novarum_en.html. The critical edition of the text is *L'enciclia Rerum Novarum: Texto authentico e redazioni preparatorie dai documenti originali*, ed. Giovanni Antonazzi (Edizione de Storia e Letteratura, 1957). Unfortunately, the numbering systems vary between the critical edition and the Vatican translation.

13. Leo XIII, *Rerum Novarum* 45.

14. Group interview with national Catholic lay leaders.

15. John Olin, *Catholic Reform: From Cardinal Ximenes to the Council of Trent* (Fordham University Press, 1990), 4–11.

16. Olin, *Catholic Reform*, 36.

17. Norman P. Tanner, ed., *Decrees of the Ecumenical Councils*, 2 vols. (Georgetown University Press, 1990), 2:751. This is contained in Canon 18 of the 23rd session.

18. We treated this in chapter 2. See Lant Pritchett and Frauke de Weijer, "Fragile States: Stuck in a Capability Trap?," World Development Report 2011 Background Paper (World Bank, 2010), 28.

19. *Program for Priestly Formation in the United States of America*, 6th ed. (United States Conference of Catholic Bishops, 2022), 142 (§361).

20. The sixth edition is somewhat better in that it makes the distinction between *should* and *must* clear. *Program for Priestly Formation*, 4 (§9): "Care has been taken in this document to limit the use of prescriptive and exhortative language to two terms. The word 'must' means that an action is required. Authorization from the competent authority is required for an exception from following the required course of action. The word 'should' means that an action is highly recommended, such that a nonarbitrary reason is necessary for the decision not to pursue this course of action."

21. Some of the material in the following pages is drawn from Christopher Bellitto and C. Colt Anderson, "Scarlett Fever: To Combat Clericalism, Reform Seminaries," *Commonweal*, April 12, 2019, 13–15.

22. Vatican Congregation for Catholic Education Letter Reporting the Apostolic Visitation to U.S. Seminaries and Houses of Priestly Formation (December 15, 2008), 2.3 accessed at https://www.usccb.org/resources/apostolic-visitation-seminaries-report-2008.

23. Group interview with university and seminary administrators and faculty members in ministry programs.

24. Congregation for the Clergy, *Ratio Fundamentalis Instructionis Sacerdotalis* (L'Osservatore Romano, 2016), §35.

25. *Ratio* (2016), §33.

26. *Program for Priestly Formation* §23 (p. 12).

27. *Ratio* (2016), §34.

28. *Ratio* (2016), §68.

29. *Ratio* (2016), §69.

30. *Ratio* (2016), §41.

31. *Ratio* (2016), §42.

32. *Ratio* (2016), §42.

33. *Ratio* (2016), §92.

34. *Ratio* (2016), §92.

35. *Ratio* (2016), §39.

36. *Ratio* (2016), §120. See also *Ratio*, §94: "In the moral sphere, it is connected to the requirement that the individual arrive gradually at a well formed conscience. This means that he will become a responsible person able to make the right decisions, gifted with right judgement and able to have an objective perception of persons and events."

37. *Ratio* (2016), §43; *PPF* §43.

38. Catherine of Siena, *The Dialogue*, 103 (195). For more on this point see C. Colt Anderson, *The Great Catholic Reformers: From Gregory the Great to Dorothy Day* (Paulist Press, 2007), 113–17.

39. Tanner, *Decrees of the Ecumenical Councils*, 2:911, 1010, 1054, 1070. These page numbers correspond to, in order: Decree on Ecumenism 4; Decree on Religious Liberty 15; Decree on the Life and Ministry of Priests 9; Pastoral Constitution on the Church in the World Today 4.

40. Gregory the Great, *Pastoral Care*, 1.2. See Anderson, *The Great Catholic Reformers*, 18–22.

41. Gregory the Great, *Pastoral Care*, 2.6.

42. Bernard of Clairvaux, *On Conversion*, 19.32, 21.38. For more see Anderson, *The Great Catholic Reformers*, 69–74.

43. Tanner, *Decrees of the Ecumenical Councils*, 2:714.

44. Tanner, *Decrees of the Ecumenical Councils*, 2:667.

45. Tanner, *Decrees of the Ecumenical Councils*, 2:675.

46. Tanner, *Decrees of the Ecumenical Councils*, 2:678.

47. *Ratio* (1970), §44; *Ratio* (1985), §44. We are using an English translation that was published as *A Basic Scheme for Priestly Training: Ratio Fundamentalis Institutionis Sacerdotalis* (The Daughters of St. Paul, 1970). Because this text may be difficult to find, we simply cite the

section numbers. There is an English translation on the internet that seems to be based on the edition we are using.

48. *Ratio* (1970), §45; *Ratio* (1985), §45.

49. *Ratio* (1970), §49; *Ratio* (1985), §49.

50. *Ratio* (2016), §69.

51. *Ratio* (1970), Introduction §3; *Ratio* (1985), introduction §3.

CONCLUSION

1. Bernard of Clairvaux, Letter 80.7. This is letter 78.7 in the critical edition. The best English translation of the letters is *The Letters of St. Bernard of Clairvaux*, trans. Bruno Scott James (Cistercian Publications, 1998; 1st ed. Burns and Oates, 1953).

2. Norman P. Tanner, ed., *Decrees of the Ecumenical Councils*, 2 vols. (Georgetown University Press, 1990), 2:875. *Lumen Gentium* 31.

3. Douglass C. North, *Institutions, Institutional Change and Economic Performance* (Cambridge University Press, 1990), 89. Other problems in the church might require change that is more revolutionary or punctuated in nature.

4. North, *Institutions*, 90.

5. We thank Robert Hurley for sharing his forthcoming article, which presents the idea that the Catholic Church suffers from a learning disability that undermines its dynamic capacity to learn and improve as an organization. The working title is "When Impediments to Learning Undermine Organisational Trust: An Exploration in the Context of the Child Sexual Abuse Crisis Within the Catholic Church."

6. John J. Burkhard, OFM Conv, *The Sense of the Faith in History: Its Sources, Reception, and Theology* (Liturgical Press, 2022).

7. Burkhard, *The Sense of the Faith in History*, 250–51. Burkhard cites *Lumen Gentium* 12 to show the dynamic aspect of the sense of the faith.

8. See chapter 1. Robert M. Cover, "The Supreme Court, 1982 Term—Foreword: Nomos and Narrative" (1983) https://www.scribd.com/document/202631569/Robert-M-Cover-The-Supreme-Court-1982-Term-Foreword-Nomos-and-Narrative/.

9. North, *Institutions*, 89.

10. John Henry Newman, *An Essay on the Development of Christian Doctrine* (Christian Classics, 1968), 40.

11. North, *Institutions*, 90.

12. Bernhard Schimmelpfennig notes that the *defensores* were minor clerics who were able to marry in *The Papacy*, trans. James Sievert (Columbia University Press, 1992), 60–61.

13. For more information see C. Colt Anderson, *The Great Catholic Reformers: From Gregory the Great to Dorothy Day* (Paulist Press, 2007), 51–53.

14. Matt Andrews, Lant Pritchett, and Michael Woolcock, "Escaping Capability Traps Through Problem-Driven Iterative Adaptation," *World Development* 51 (2013): 234–44.

15. Andrews, Pritchett, and Woolcock, "Escaping Capability," 237.

16. Andrews, Pritchett, and Woolcock, "Escaping Capability," 238–39.

17. Fourth Lateran Council, Canon 30 in Tanner, *Decrees of the Ecumenical Councils*, 1:249: "It is very serious and absurd that prelates [bishops] of churches, when they can promote suitable men to ecclesiastical benefices, are not afraid to choose unworthy men who lack both learning and honesty of behavior and who follow the urgings of the flesh rather than the judgment of reason. Nobody of sound mind is ignorant of how much damage to churches arises from this....Therefore he who has been found guilty after a first and second correction is to be suspended from conferring ecclesiastical benefices by the provincial council, and a prudent and honest person is to be appointed at the same council to make up for the suspended person's failure."

18. This section summarizes C. Colt Anderson, "The Problem with Hierarchy Today," *New Theology Review* (2007): 25–33.

19. Pseudo-Dionysius the Areopagite, *Celestial Hierarchy*, 3.1. There are several English translations, but we are using *Pseudo-Dionysius: The Complete Works*, ed. and trans. Colm Luibhéid and Paul Rorem (Paulist Press, 1987).

20. Pseudo-Dionysius the Areopagite, *Ecclesiastical Hierarchy*, 5.1–6.3.

21. Pseudo-Dionysius the Areopagite, *Celestial Hierarchy*, 3.2.

22. Pseudo-Dionysius the Areopagite, *Celestial Hierarchy*, 2.3.

23. See Tanner, *Decrees of the Ecumenical Councils*, 2:862–74. *Lumen Gentium* 18–29.

24. Bonaventure, *Collations on the Six Days*, 20.14–20. The newest English translation is *Conferences on the Six Days*, trans. and ed. Jay M. Hammond (Franciscan Institute Publications, 2018).

25. This section draws upon C. Colt Anderson, "Recovering the Apologetics of Humility," *New Theology Review* (2010): 25–34.

26. Augustine, *De doctrina christiana*, 3.31.44–3.32.45. There are multiple English translations, but we use Augustine, *Teaching Christianity: De doctrina christiana*, trans. Edmund Hill, OP, ed. John E. Rotelle, OSA (New City Press, 1996).

27. Jeffrey Richards, *Consul of God: The Life and Times of Gregory the Great* (Routledge & Kegan Paul, 1980), 108–24.

28. Gregory the Great, *Moral Reflections on the Book of Job*, vol. 1, trans. Brian Kerns, OCSO (Liturgical Press, 2014), 69.

29. Gregory the Great, *Moral Reflections on the Book of Job*, 1:71.

30. Gregory the Great, *Pastoral Care*, trans. Henry Davis, SJ (Newman Press, 1950), 108–9.

31. Gregory the Great, *Moral Reflections on the Book of Job*, 1:219.

32. Tanner, *Decrees of the Ecumenical Councils*, 2:855. *Lumen Gentium* 8.

INDEX